What people are saying about *Hope for an Unwa*

These are biblically based devotionals refined by the incurable *love* ⟨...⟩ nourished by deepening *faith*, and anchored in the enduring *hope* in ⟨...⟩. Brutally open and honest! Spiritually refreshing for any reader!

—Rev. Dr. T.V. Thomas
Chairman, Lausanne Global Diaspora Network (GDN)

This is a devotional book long overdue—a volume of biblical insight, wise counsel, and helpful prayers for those broken by the brokenness of the people they love. Written by seasoned veterans touched personally by the raging wars of addiction and who have lived in the trenches with many wounded, each daily reading points clearly to the One who binds up the broken-hearted and can set the captives free.

—John Mahaffey
Lead Pastor, West Highland Baptist Church, Hamilton, Ontario
Council member of The Gospel Coalition in Canada

Hope for an Unwanted Journey is an honest and deeply personal glimpse into a mom and dad's imperfect but tireless effort to love and support their son caught in the entanglement of addiction. The reader is invited into a reflective exploration of the many haunting questions and issues at play through a daily devotional journal. Rather than offering simple or trite answers, the rhythms of scripture engagement and prayer are modelled. The intentional looking to a "higher power" found ultimately in Jesus is shown to be the spark of hope the authors discovered on their tumultuous journey. Those who find themselves on a similar path, awash in pain and confusion, will discover soulmates in Donna and Bill. Like the journey itself, digesting the insights contained within, slowly and reflectively, will reap the richest result.

—Ed Willms
Former Executive Director of the Ontario MB Conference of Churches

When I heard that Bill and Donna were preparing a book dealing with this subject matter, I knew it would be an important read. Anything written by people with their kind of credibility always is. *Hope for an Unwanted Journey* was everything I expected, and more. Their gifted writing blends a casual style that makes for very easy reading with profound insights powerfully relevant for us all. This is a valuable resource, not just for those struggling to uphold a loved one lost in addiction and/or mental illness, but for anyone seeking to maintain a healthy Christ-centred focus through a time of spiritual weariness. Their courage in sharing has been a wonderful gift to me and others.

—Doug Hammond
Commanding Officer of Bloor Central Community Church, Salvation Army

For families and loved ones who are on this unwanted journey, we are confident that this devotional will bring hope, healing, and encouragement wherever readers find themselves. This book calls us to dig deep and look to the One from whom our help comes. The pages are not full of platitudes but rather promises from our Father in heaven, who is always faithful. Thank you to Donna and Bill for sensitively writing this much-needed book that will be a lifeline to many.

—Pastor Phil and Michelle Collins
Willow Park Church, Kelowna

Donna and Bill Dyck invite us to join them in a very intimate, raw, and profoundly honest journey into the emotional rollercoaster of caring for a loved one who is suffering from a devastating addiction. Having lived this journey ourselves, it was so healing to be given words to what we were feeling and thinking. So often we felt like we were going crazy living between hope and despair, fear and courage, and doubt and belief.

Using a devotional format, the authors masterfully draw their readers into the hidden places of the soul and expose the most vulnerable and fragile emotions. It is in that place, where denial is removed and permission to grieve is given, that the grace of Jesus is not just understood but experienced. This is a must-read for every family caught in the trauma of an unwanted journey and desperately longing to experience hope that is real, lasting, and healing.

—Rev. Dr. David Hearn
Senior Associate Pastor of Kamloops Alliance Church

Through a delicate blend of Scripture and heartfelt prayers, Bill and Donna provide not only profound encouragement but a vehicle for expressing those emotions that are beyond words when one's child is in the relentless grip of an addiction. Their journey reminds us that there is a hope, and that there is a healer.

—Rev. William (Bill) R. McAlpine, Ph.D
Retired Professor Emeritus, Ambrose University

This book breathes so much *hope* regarding any unwanted journey you may be travelling. Each and every day, our hearts are saturated with Scripture, refocused on Him, and ended in prayer. A must-read.

—Marie Joynt
Speaker, teacher blogger

This journaled devotional is a gift. Bill and Donna understand the emotion, questions, and compassion one experiences when living with an addict. The biblical and parental insight is sincere, honest, and truthful. You will more than read this journal; you will interact with God-centred counsel, wisdom, and experience while walking away with humble confidence that God is in control.

—Rev. Tim Moore, DMin

Daily Readings for Those Whose Loved Ones Struggle with Addiction/Mental Illness

HOPE
for an Unwanted Journey

BILL & DONNA LEA DYCK

HOPE FOR AN UNWANTED JOURNEY
Copyright © 2023 by Bill and Donna Lea Dyck

Cover art by Bärbel Smith, SCA, OSA, AFCA
Contemporary Canadian Landscape Artist, www.barbelsmith.com

All rights reserved. Neither this publication nor any part of this publication may be reproduced or transmitted in any form or by any means, electronic or mechanical, including photocopying, recording or any information storage and retrieval system, without permission in writing from the author.

Scripture quotations are from the ESV® Bible (The Holy Bible, English Standard Version®), copyright © 2001 by Crossway, a publishing ministry of Good News Publishers. Used by permission. All rights reserved. The ESV text may not be quoted in any publication made available to the public by a Creative Commons license. The ESV may not be translated in whole or in part into any other language. Scripture quotations marked (NLT) are taken from the Holy Bible, New Living Translation, copyright ©1996, 2004, 2015 by Tyndale House Foundation. Used by permission of Tyndale House Publishers, a Division of Tyndale House Ministries, Carol Stream, Illinois 60188. All rights reserved. Scripture quotations marked (NIV) are taken from the Holy Bible, New International Version®, NIV®. Copyright © 1973, 1978, 1984, 2011 by Biblica, Inc.™ Used by permission of Zondervan. All rights reserved worldwide. www.zondervan.comThe "NIV" and "New International Version" are trademarks registered in the United States Patent and Trademark Office by Biblica, Inc.™

Print ISBN: 978-1-4866-2267-2 | Hardcover ISBN: 978-1-4866-2391-4
eBook ISBN: 978-1-4866-2268-9

Word Alive Press
119 De Baets Street, Winnipeg, MB R2J 3R9
www.wordalivepress.ca

Cataloguing in Publication may be obtained through Library and Archives Canada

This book is dedicated to every parent or individual who must walk this unwanted journey. May you find hope and encouragement within its pages.

CONTENTS

Acknowledgements	xi
Dear Reader	xiii
Foreword	xv

Week I: Moving Beyond Worry Prayer
1. Giving Thanks! Seriously? — 1
2. Why Waiting Matters — 2
3. Where to Rest Your Weary Soul — 3
4. Crying Out to God! — 4
5. Truly Leaving Your Cares with God — 5

Week II: The Battle of Forgiveness
1. Forgive Often — 9
2. Forgiveness: The Only Way Forward — 10
3. Why Forgiveness Matters — 11
4. Finding the Strength to Forgive — 12
5. How Forgiveness Improves Your Situation — 13

Week III: The Indispensable Place of Thanksgiving
1. A Pathway to God's Presence — 17
2. A Pathway to Experiencing God's Promises — 18
3. A Key to Finding God's Peace — 19
4. A Mighty Spiritual Weapon — 20
5. A Beautiful Offering to God — 21

Week IV: Finding Courage for Complicated Decisions
1. Called to Courage — 25
2. How to Acquire Courage — 26
3. How to Explain Courage — 27
4. How Knowledge Builds Courage — 28
5. Why Courage Matters — 29

Week V: Overcoming Numbness
1. The Dangers of Forgetting — 33
2. Breathe in God's Word — 34
3. Fresh Pathways to the Heart — 35
4. God's Got It in Hand — 36
5. God and God Alone — 37

Week VI: Finding Hope in the Ditch of Despair
1. The Anatomy of Hope — 41
2. Focus on the Long Game — 42
3. The Source of Hope — 43
4. The Essence of Hope — 44
5. The Strength of Hope — 45

Week VII: Seeing Beyond the Brokenness
1. A Desperate Peace — 49
2. Pointed Prayers — 50
3. Determined to Live — 51
4. A Favourable Outcome — 52
5. Keep Moving — 53

Week VIII: The Ever-Present Promises of God
1. The Unfailing Presence of God — 57
2. Kept by God — 58
3. Helped by God — 59
4. Strengthened by God — 60
5. Led by God — 61

Week IX: Pursuing Peace When Fear Is Near
1. When God Seems Unconcerned — 65
2. Powerful Peace — 66
3. Peace Knowing God Hears Our Prayers — 67
4. Peace Knowing You Matter to God — 68
5. Kept in Peace by God — 69

Week X: The Control Factor
1. Unpacking the Urge to Rescue — 73
2. So What Is God's Part and What Is Mine? — 74
3. Misguided Compassion — 75
4. Love Versus the Control Factor — 76
5. Playing God — 77

Week XI: Holding onto Faith
1. Faith that Brings a Loved One to Jesus — 81
2. Who Exactly Are You Trusting? — 82
3. Holding Steady Amid Bad News — 83
4. It's a Matter of Asking — 84
5. Wait for the Lord — 85

Week XII: Within God's Reach
1. Don't Disqualify Yourself — 89
2. Trusting God When Things Look Impossible — 90
3. Identifying What Keeps Us from Experiencing God's Deliverance — 91
4. God Is That Great — 92
5. Crying Out to God — 93

Week XIII: Hopeful Living Alongside the Mentally Ill
1. Why Making God Your Refuge Is Vital — 97
2. A Measured Response — 98
3. Finding a Safe Place — 99
4. There Is Purpose to Your Pain — 100
5. Moving the Goal Posts — 101

Week XIV: God's Wisdom in the Sea of Confusion
1. Why Wait for Joy? — 105
2. The Non-Deserter — 106
3. Figuring out the Mess — 107
4. Order out of Chaos — 108
5. Manage Your Gaze — 109

Week XV: Putting Anger in Its Place
1. Quick to Hear — 113
2. Slow to Become Angry — 114
3. Pursue Words of Healing — 115
4. There's More at Stake Than You Think — 116
5. Choose Gentleness — 117

Week XVI: Overcoming Evil
1. Jesus, Greater Than All — 121
2. The Love and Power of Jesus — 122
3. Breaking Strongholds — 123
4. The Value of Small Faith — 124
5. Becoming Battle Ready — 125

Week XVII: A Long Wait in the Right Direction
1. Troubleshooting Exhaustion — 129
2. The Value of Gazing Upon Beauty — 130
3. Finding Strength in the Journey of Others — 131
4. Living for an Eternal Reward — 132
5. Finding Contentment — 133

Week XVIII: Wound Care for Toxic Conversations
1. The Anatomy of Toxic Words — 137
2. Where Vindication Comes From — 138
3. Finding Freedom from Toxic Words — 139
4. Discerning the Right Season — 140
5. The Value of Being Slow to Anger — 141

Week XIX: Understanding Selfishness

1. Overcoming Our Own Selfishness . 145
2. Understanding Compulsion 146
3. How to Keep Loving Amid a Climate of Entitlement 147
4. A Precious Toolbox 148
5. Overcoming Amid Opposition 149

Week XX: The Power of Prayer and Fasting

1. How to Handle Devastating News 153
2. Fasting: the Key to Going Deeper 154
3. Fasting: How to Navigate an Evil Day 155
4. Fasting for the Presence of God 156
5. The Reward of Fasting 157

Week XXI: Choosing Our Words Determines Our Way

1. Why Hopeful Words Matter 161
2. When Thankfulness Is a Hard Choice 162
3. Benefits to Letting Your Words Lead You to a Different Place 163
4. There's So Much at Risk 164
5. The Impact of Scripture on Our Words 165

Week XXII: Who Takes Centre Stage, God or Your Loved One?

1. The Value of Sitting with Jesus 169
2. How to Stay Centred on God 170
3. Don't Wait for Things to Improve 171
4. Ways That God Helps Us Stay Centred on Him 172
5. Keeping Our Hope Fixed on God Alone 173

Week XXIII: The Folly of Presumption

1. Fighting Against Bad News 177
2. How to Find Hope When Nobody Else Does 178
3. The Presumption of Storms 179
4. The Presumption of Predicting Outcome 180
5. How to Think about Things Future 181

Week XXIV: A Holy Partnership

1. Trusting the Potter with the Clay 185
2. Gaining Wisdom from God 186
3. Entering into Christ's Compassion 187
4. Overcoming Obstacles 188
5. Receiving Help from God 189

About the Authors 191
About the Artist 193

ACKNOWLEDGEMENTS

We want to acknowledge all of our family and friends who stood by us as we walked this journey. Your love and prayers will never be forgotten. We deeply appreciate each one of you. We also acknowledge the impact of Church Renewal (CR), whose weekly mentoring has been a great support. Though quoted nowhere, the thought of CR discipleship is reflected in many of the writings. Above all, we acknowledge our Heavenly Father who led, comforted, and sustained us daily.

DEAR READER

This book has been written to bring encouragement and hope to parents with loved ones ensnared by addiction. For all of us, it is an unwanted journey. Nobody goes looking for that experience. It simply comes to us. Whatever road we're on becomes significantly altered because our loved one has fallen into this great entanglement.

We cannot ignore it because of its seriousness, nor would we want to. So much is at stake. Our love for them demands a course correction on our part in order to walk with them.

The difficulty is that while there's often quite of bit of help available to the one addicted, should they wish to embrace it, there is little for the person who loves that addict. Yet the struggles are massive and the questions penetrating. We feel like fish out of water. Many of us have never felt this way before. Our relationship with our loved one suddenly seems profoundly superficial because of our inability to connect meaningfully with them. We struggle to find solid footing. The result is deep discouragement all around.

This is why we seek to bring encouragement and hope, particularly to the parents of the one addicted.

Compulsion is altogether terrible, both for our loved ones as well as for those who live next to them. Simplistic solutions don't do justice to the gravity of the situation. Trying to stop addiction is like standing in front of a loaded tractor trailer speeding towards you and thinking that your raised hand is going to do it.

We have lived with it in our family for many years and also walked with countless addicts in our church outreaches in downtown Toronto.

We do not, however, claim to be experts on addiction. We have learnt much in this journey and are always learning. We wouldn't contradict the words of medical practitioners and those who truly are experts in the field. The purpose of this book is not to prescribe strategies to see the one addicted come free, much as we desire that. We don't offer ten easy steps to attain freedom from addiction.

We do, however, share many lessons learnt along the way. There are things to be avoided which undermine a person's healing; these we are eager to share. There are also practices to embrace, which when put into place are helpful in seeing our loved ones come free. Our thinking needs to be adjusted on many counts so that we become part of the solution.

To a lesser extent, the book addresses issues of mental illness. In our experience, mental illness is not far away when addiction is present. This is one of the reasons that addiction is so complex and seeing people come free of it so challenging.

Yet there is hope—and it is found in God.

The book is written as a devotional: to lend a spiritual perspective and tools for walking this journey with your loved one. Questions rise amid the great suffering of those who live alongside an addicted person. For example, "Where is God in the middle of all this? What is he saying to me? What did I do wrong? What should I do next? Is there hope for my loved one?"

Each entry is based on a specific passage of Scripture following topics we felt crucial to the conversation. God wants to encourage you, dear reader, to bring you hope and a way forward in your relationship with your loved one. He is near and will guide you through this unwanted journey. Though the way is unfamiliar to you, it is not to him.

As you read through this book, the voice is Donna's, but Bill has come behind each entry and made his contribution. The writing is from both of us. This devotional is something we each felt led by God to do.

This is not a devotional written on a beach, with the sun shining. While we are writing on the other side of the journey, we address those who are living it. Many portions of this were difficult to write, as forgetting it all would have been so much easier. If you, though, our readers, will benefit from something we learned and find encouragement, it will have been well worth it.

The book is not about our loved one and his journey in addiction. It is about us and lessons we learned along the way. In it we share details of those years of struggle only insofar as they may be helpful.

Please know that our son has given us permission to speak as we do. At the time of this writing, he has been sober for five years, and for this we thank God daily. While we are so proud of his many accomplishments, our greatest joy has to do with his freedom from alcohol, which was destroying his life.

Donna's brother and father also struggled with addiction. Neither of them overcame the compulsion and died young as a result. There is so much at risk. Victories are to be greatly celebrated, however small, on this unwanted journey.

May God bring comfort to your heart and fill you with hope as you read.

Sincerely,
Bill and Donna Lea Dyck

P.S. If you want to communicate with Donna or Bill, please visit Donna's website: www.donnaleadyck.com

FOREWORD

I am the "loved one" Bill and Donna reference throughout this book. On this date of writing, I am 1,984 days (about five and a half years) clean and sober.

In the pages that follow, my parents lay out in a devotional format what it was like—and in some cases, what it presently is like—to walk with me, and to have walked with my uncle and grandfather through our respective substance addictions. They offer a deeply personal and spiritual reflection on the challenges they faced in an effort to offer hope and direction to anyone who is on a similar journey to their own.

I must confess, the perceptions and recollections of the events recounted by my parents are sometimes different than my own. This is to be expected. I acknowledge that I didn't have an accurate grasp of reality while I was deep in alcoholism and severe mental illness. This, however, doesn't belittle or negate my own recollections of past events or elevate those of my parents. It's simply an aspect of the complexity that is addiction and substance abuse on the part of the sufferer. At the end of the day, I still need to deal with my own perceptions and interpretations of past events and the associated emotional fallout. Delusional or not, grace met me.

What is certain, coming from my years in addiction, is that a great deal of pain was felt by all. Much of the pain, if not the majority, was a direct consequence of my actions. I was at points sickened by the words I read as I went through the present manuscript. In fairness, my parents share only enough detail of a particular story to get the point across, and for that I am grateful. As you the reader are probably aware, addiction and substance abuse are messy, painful, and at times gut-wrenching.

I am convinced that this book by my parents will be of benefit to those who travel(led) a similar road. There is no shortage of literature and programs available for the suffering alcoholic and addict, but there is so little that is accessible for the family. They offer here a bold approach to those who walk with loved ones struggling with substance dependencies.

My prayers are with you, reader. May the Lord meet you where you are. May the grace that found me find you and your loved one.

—the loved one

MOVING BEYOND WORRY PRAYER
Week One
Introduction

One day I was driving and thinking about my loved one—nothing new, really. He was never far from my mind. I battled the fear that he would be out drinking again, or worse, take too many pills and try to end his struggle.

I know that no addict is excited about their addiction. Some walk in it with buddies who give little thought to their lives and where they're headed. Others are at a place where they want to break free, but it isn't easy.

I have never struggled with addictions, but I have seen enough to say that overcoming one isn't as simple as deciding one day that the battle is over for all time. It's often a struggle that remains for the rest of a person's life. Sobriety is achieved one day at a time. Recovering alcoholics and drug addicts are among the bravest and most determined people I know.

On this particular day, while driving home from work and praying for our son, I asked God to be with him and help him. The truth is that my prayer went in circles as I repeated myself over and over.

Several kilometres later, while I was sitting at a red light, the Lord spoke to me: *"Donna, you are not praying; you are just worrying in prayer form."*

And it was true. I wasn't releasing my worries or fears. Rather, I was instructing God over and over about what I wanted him to do. What I had was not faith; instead it was a shaky hope.

The word of God says to all of us that the prayer spoken in faith can move mountains. My prayer was not even able to move the dust from my dashboard, let alone a mountain. Before me was a huge mountain that needed desperately to move!

GIVING THANKS! SERIOUSLY?

Day One

Read James 1:2–8

Count it all joy… when you meet trials of various kinds, for you know that the testing of your faith produces steadfastness… If any of you lacks wisdom, let him ask God, who gives generously to all without reproach, and it will be given him.

—James 1:2–3, 5

As I read this passage, I find it difficult to accept. How can one consider this journey to be joyful and wholeheartedly say, "Thanks so much for making me go through this, God" with any level of sincerity?

Is God asking me to say "Thank you" for the heartbreaking events of this journey that a loved one struggling with addiction/mental illness is on? Doubtful! Rather, we can thank God for the way he uses terrible things to shape us and remind us of how desperately we need him, daily.

We can also be thankful for the way he is building tenacity in us. We wish to be done with this dreadful affliction on our loved one in a moment. Just because that's not the case doesn't mean God is not working. So we patiently pray with all steadfastness, never losing hope, never withdrawing love. God is pleased with that. That is a great climate for Him to work in.

We must also be thankful for the invitation to ask God for wisdom regarding this trial we find ourselves in (James 1:5). We need that daily because we don't know the way through this difficulty.

So much about addiction and mental illness requires wisdom and insight far beyond what we possess. People with these struggles have eyes that see the world differently. They encounter events and people in a way we do not understand. It leaves us baffled. In addition, we need to know what God is doing and where he is in this difficulty we face. He is certainly working, but where? Will he not speak to us, comforting us, giving us hope and direction? Yes, he will.

Asking of God and receiving from God are both privileges given to us (James 1:5, 7)—not just one, but both. I have not always found God to be quick in telling me exactly what I need to know, but he does come through. His word says that he will and I choose to receive this today.

Dear Father,
You see what I cannot. Lead me step by step. Give to me wisdom for today, whatever it holds.
Meet me in the good of this day and in the not-so-good. Give me a sense of your presence.
Watch over my loved one, Father. I need you to save them.
In Jesus's name, amen.

WHY WAITING MATTERS
Day Two
Read Psalm 5:1–3

Listen to my voice in the morning, Lord. Each morning I bring my requests to you and wait expectantly.
—Psalm 5:3, NLT

To begin one's day, laying down every burden or haunting memory is an excellent strategy; all awful conversations, each impossible circumstance, all of it. It certainly beats complaining or rehearsing it repeatedly. That accomplishes little, though I confess that the temptation to do it is great. There is a time to talk to friends and family, but it never replaces laying it all down before God himself each day.

When I was walking through some of the deepest parts of the valley in this journey, I had to remember just who it was inviting me to lay out my requests. This was not an invitation given by one who overpromises and underdelivers or one who is weak and unable to see beyond the next required step.

No—this is our God, the creator of the universe. His wisdom knows no limit. Nothing is unseen by him. He can be where I cannot. He can do what I am not able to. He hears our requests and teaches us to wait in expectation.

He is with us in the waiting, for he gives us peace in the middle of terrible situations. He helps us think when normally it would be impossible to do so. His presence quiets us. It is never an empty waiting devoid of his presence. Neither is it an anxious waiting, for if we have asked, he has heard. To bring our requests to him each morning is not to relive our anxiety but to allow our hearts to be quieted by the fact that he hears us and is therefore at work. We must wait confidently and expectantly.

One more thing: what are we waiting for? Who are you waiting for? It's easy for us to fix our eyes on our loved one and wait for them to change, which will only increase our anxiety and put strain on the relationship. Rather, we wait for God. When he acts, it is done.

I have never been good at waiting, yet so much of life is lived there. Maybe that is you. God says to lay out our requests before him and then wait. Just wait. Wait on the Lord.

Dear Father,
You know my list, my requests. You hear the desperation in my voice. Thank you that nothing you have heard from my list of requests is alarming to you. As I have laid them out before you, I ask that you help me to truly wait in expectation.
In Jesus's name, amen.

WHERE TO REST YOUR WEARY SOUL
Day Three
Read Psalm 33:13–22

Behold, the eye of the Lord is on those who fear him, on those who hope in his steadfast love…

—Psalm 33:18

This world offers no end of solutions to our every problem. Some work, many do not. When it comes to alcoholism, there is a medication one can take that will curb the desire to drink. My son used to call it "flu in a bottle." It wasn't hard for me to put hope in this drug. He took it off and on for weeks, months. It never addressed the real problem, though—why he drank—nor was it what made him finally stop.

This passage declares that God sees all (Psalm 33:13–15). Not only does this mean that nothing escapes his notice but that he understands perfectly why our loved ones do what they do and what it will take for them to stop. It often takes people a while to understand why they do what they do. We ourselves struggle to figure out what is at the root of the problem. God has it perfectly in hand. That's why we need to wait quietly for him; he helps us understand things we would never come to on our own.

In addition, God talks about rescue (Psalm 33:16–17). That's what we're interested in, isn't it? Sadly, our insights, strength, and many interventions aren't going to save the day. All we may truly be able to do is sit, wait, and try not to pull our hair out!

I had to choose to trust God, even though from my human eyes I saw plenty of reason to despair. I could see no real signs of recovery, and definitely little faith in my loved one's life.

However, I chose to trust in the unfailing love of God. Here I find rest for my weary soul. I don't know where else I can go. I'm sure that sitting on a nice warm beach would help! Yet that would only last for as long as I sat there. I need something I can take with me wherever I go. God alone has the power to save—both my loved one and me. I choose to hope in him.

Dear Father,
You see the turmoil of my heart and all we are going through. My hope is simply in your unfailing love. Here I rest. Make me more aware of your steadfast love no matter what happens. Intervene in the life of my loved one. Thank you for your presence. I could not walk this path without you.
In Jesus's name, amen.

CRYING OUT TO GOD!
Day Four
Read Psalm 18:1–6

In my distress I called upon the Lord; to my God I cried for help. From his temple he heard my voice, and my cry to him reached his ears.

—Psalm 18:6

I have always found it comforting to sit in a coffee shop with a friend who really listens and understands me. There's a difference between this very understanding friend and God; God has power and wisdom infinitely beyond anything a person possesses.

It is comforting to remember that God is very different from people. As a young mom, I would sometimes tune my kids out when they came to me with their endless requests. I heard them, but sometimes it went in one ear and out the other. I am so thankful that God isn't like that.

Psalm 18:6 reminds us that in our distress, we call out to God. Anyone can do that. That's not to say that we actually do, though. There are many things we can choose to do in our distress outside of calling out to God. Simply directing our pain and anxiety towards him in an honest cry for help is unquestionably the most profitable course. It's a cry. There's desperation in it and great urgency. We feel such dependence and vulnerability in that moment. But cry we must, cry out to God for help.

The Bible states then that God listens to our cry. Do you need that reminder? God hears your voice; your cry reaches his ears. Don't say that your prayers ricochet off the ceiling. When you cry in desperation to God for help, Scripture says that he hears your voice and acts. The one who is infinite in power has heard your cry.

Now, that brings a sigh of relief! We need such assurance. We need him. Peace will only come as you acknowledge this truth and then cry out to him!

Dear Father,
Thank you for hearing me when I call to you. I have such fear and apprehension over the life of my loved one. Reach down and intervene. Give me peace and strength for today. I need you to watch over my loved one. You can do that like no one else.
In Jesus's name, amen.

TRULY LEAVING YOUR CARES WITH GOD
Day Five
Read 1 Peter 5:6–7

Give all your worries and cares to God, for he cares about you.

—1 Peter 5:7, NLT

It's easy to hold onto what haunts us. I don't need instructions on how to do that, especially for my loved one.

When a drunken text lit up my phone, my heart would begin to race, and then the panic would set in. This was generally the order of things. I wish I could say this only happened sometimes, but that would be a lie. I had well-meaning friends say, "Donna, you shouldn't worry." If only it was that simple.

One of the best ways in which I can truly give my cares to God and leave them with him is to believe that he is powerful and loving enough to indeed care for my loved one. I need to know that in the middle of the messiness of my son's life, my Lord, my Good Shepherd, will truly be with him, every moment. Then I must say "Thank you," as that is the appropriate way of acknowledging that God has it all in hand.

While I know that I may not be able to trust my loved one in his current state, I can trust God who holds the world in his hands. He who is all-wise and whose power knows no limits stands near my loved one. It's probably impossible to truly give our cares to God if we don't believe he is trustworthy or able to actually carry them.

Nothing about this is easy, but it's possible. Whatever the worry or care, God says we ought to give it to him. There is something deeply comforting in the knowledge that the one to whom we are passing this desperate worry cares for us. Giving the care of a loved one to someone who cares deeply is so much more comforting than passing that precious loved one to someone who is indifferent. God is *not* indifferent. He loves and cares for us and for our loved one. His greatness is without limit and he is faithful.

Dear Father,
I lay my loved one down before you today. I want to say thank you for caring for me and for this loved one who is dear to my heart. You know all my fears and see where my loved one is right now. Watch over him. Care for him in all the ways I cannot. I so much want to rescue him, but I am unable to do that. This truth frustrates me so deeply. I come to you and continue to ask: watch over my loved one today, wherever he is. Thank you for hearing my prayer. In Jesus's name, amen.

THE BATTLE OF FORGIVENESS
Week Two
Introduction

If an addict or someone you love who struggles with mental illness frequently brings you anything, it's the opportunity to be offended, hurt, or wronged. I remember that money was taken from me several times without my permission or knowledge.

In addition, terrible things will be said to you, especially when they're under the influence of a substance. I remember people saying to me, "Remember, it's the alcohol speaking." Frankly, that never helped me. It sounded good, but I found little comfort in it.

As I look back on when I was a kid dealing with my father and his drinking, I remember that he said and did some terrible things. He provided all kinds of opportunities for me to resent him. The same can be said about my brother, who did some foolish things that had a huge impact on our family.

Our own loved one then presented a whole new set of challenges.

It's not easy to forgive these people, but choosing not to forgive doesn't help them—and it certainly doesn't help us.

Unforgiveness turns into bitterness, which becomes a poison that alters the way we see life. Not just where our loved one is concerned, but other people as well. Bitterness does not lessen over the years; it grows. It behaves like an undetected cancer, except that it's in the soul.

I learned long ago that I had to repeatedly forgive my dad, my brother, and eventually our own adult child.

This practice of forgiveness isn't for the benefit of the person who has hurt you so much as it's for the person who extends it. Forgiveness is certainly a gift to receive, but it is also a gift to give. One that will set you free.

FORGIVE OFTEN
Day One
Read Luke 17:1–19

If your brother sins, rebuke him, and if he repents, forgive him, and if he sins against you seven times in the day, and turns to you seven times, saying, "I repent," you must forgive him.

—Luke 17:3–4

Some alcoholics are full of regret and repentance the day after. That has been our experience. They certainly can come humbly and full of promises at that point. Even while I would accept the heartfelt apology, I knew the promises wouldn't last, that this entire scene would be rehearsed again in a few days.

I would go through such a mix of emotions. Frankly, I would simply be thankful he was still alive and had made it home safely. When the apology came, on top of everything, I was often tired and had a bad headache. I slept poorly on nights when I knew he was out drinking.

When I read Luke 17, I don't read of any exceptions. It doesn't name the offence. Neither does it say that one is exempt from the obligation to forgive because of weariness, headaches, or any such thing.

Jesus instructs us that we are to forgive, even if it comes with remorse, seven times for the same sin in a single day. One would have to believe that the apology couldn't have been very heartfelt if they are back seven times in one day. I believe the point Jesus is making is simply that we are to forgive—to let it go.

It is curious that in the very next verse, the disciples ask the Lord to increase their faith, as if living so generously with forgiveness requires considerably more faith than any of them possess. Jesus, however, says to them that they have enough faith (Luke 17:6). The issue is rather one of obedience (Luke 17:7–10).

If we wait until we feel like offering forgiveness, it may not happen. We will feel the joy in the act of forgiveness as we give it freely. We are called to forgive amid our suffering. By extending forgiveness, you aren't being depleted but filled up. It may not happen immediately, but it will come.

Dear Father,
You ask much of me today. I choose to forgive my loved one for all his many hurts and offenses. I yield to you the anger and disappointment. I don't wait to feel it but choose the way of grace even as you are gracious with me. Thank you for helping me to forgive fully in this very moment.
In Jesus's name, amen.

FORGIVENESS: THE ONLY WAY FORWARD

Day Two

Read Matthew 6:14–15

For if you forgive others their trespasses, your heavenly Father will also forgive you, but if you do not forgive others their trespasses, neither will your Father forgive your trespasses.

—Matthew 6:14–15

Jesus's word to us today is that we are to forgive, period. We wish there were some wiggle room, but it won't be found. The directive is clear: we must forgive.

Resentments held onto, interestingly, are a powerful engine that drives many addicts. Hurts and offenses have built up and become something of a fortification in the soul. Until they learn to forgive, as an ongoing practice in life, it is unlikely that they will come free of their addiction. They in turn cause hurt and offense. As they were hurt, they hurt others—and usually the people they love most. It's not necessarily their intention. They are simply bearing the inevitable fruit of a tree whose root is called offense and bitterness. This is not said to excuse them, but understanding the why perhaps makes it easier to bear.

How will they come free if you respond to them in the same manner? In that case, the home just fills up with more offenses and resentments. It becomes such a toxic environment, unenjoyable for everyone. Someone must stop and simply forgive. Could it be you?

An old English poet, Alexander Pope, said, "To err is human; forgiveness is divine." We rely deeply on the forgiveness God extends to us through Christ. We learn to forgive because he forgives us so generously.

It is such a rich privilege to experience the complete forgiveness of sins. Unquestionably, forgiveness is divine. However, Christ teaches us that as we have been forgiven, so must we forgive. And that to fail to forgive is to nullify our own forgiveness. We ourselves are the ones who lose out when we fail to forgive. Alternately, to forgive opens the way for a very different flavour to enter the home which will then become life to your loved one.

Some offenses for which people ask forgiveness are inconsequential compared to things an addict says and does. That is why we need the help God offers to us.

Dear Father,
Once again, I am reminded of your requirement that I forgive people. Difficult as it may be, I choose to forgive. Forgive me for my resentments. Set me free from an unforgiving spirit. As I was forgiven, so I forgive. Heal my many hurts so I don't live out of them. Fill me with your love, kindness, and grace, for mine has run out. Thank you, Father.
In Jesus's name, amen.

WHY FORGIVENESS MATTERS
Day Three
Read Mark 11:20–25

Therefore I tell you, whatever you ask in prayer, believe that you have received it, and it will be yours. And whenever you stand praying, forgive, if you have anything against anyone, so that your Father also who is in heaven may forgive you your trespasses.

—Mark 11:24–25

Many farmhouses have mud rooms. When you come into the house, you take off your shoes and coat. The shoes are usually lined up, unless of course there are so many in which case they become a messy pile.

In today's reading, Jesus comes to a fig tree that has no fruit and he curses it. The curse is not a temper tantrum but an illustration of the judgment that will come to those who don't possess the fruit God is looking for from them.

When the disciples comment to Jesus on the now-withered fig tree the next morning, he speaks to them of bearing fruit in their lives. Fruit will be a function of what we pray for, Jesus says. And nothing will keep us from prayer like unforgiveness. Rather than reaching out to God in trusting prayer, knowing that he will definitely hear and act, we retell ourselves the latest offense by our loved one. We cannot pray in that case because we are so hurt or angry. It is a grudge. It completely replaces quiet, trusting prayer.

Consider today, what is the state of your "grudge room"? I took some time to reflect on mine. I was a little surprised at how crowded it had become in there. My collection of disappointments and frustrations with people have a way of turning open space into a grudge storage room.

Yet according to this passage, we are not allowed to keep a grudge room. No storage allowed, and for good reason. We are clearly warned that grudges have a way of hindering our prayers.

Take some time today and clean out that grudge room! The cleaning solution for this job is forgiving that individual, which we know isn't always easy, but God promises us His assistance!

Dear Father,
Thank you for your Holy Spirit, who shows me what resentments I have been storing up in my grudge room. I stand before each person today and say, "In Jesus's name, I forgive you." Father, would you go into this room now and clean it out with your love and grace? Wipe every shelf clean. Help me, O God, to keep this room empty! I don't want anything to hinder my prayers.
In Jesus's name, amen.

FINDING THE STRENGTH TO FORGIVE
Day Four
Read Colossians 3:12–14

Put on then, as God's chosen ones, holy and beloved, compassionate hearts, kindness, humility, meekness, and patience, bearing with one another and, if one has a complaint against another, forgiving each other; as the Lord has forgiven you, so you also must forgive. And above all these put on love, which binds everything together in perfect harmony.

—Colossians 3:12–14

When life is really hard, I find it more difficult to remember that as God's child I am indeed dearly loved. The fact of God's great love for each of us is easy to lose sight of. Remembering this truth, however, does make the rest of these verses a bit more palatable, especially as we must deal with difficult people.

When we need to forgive a loved one yet again, it's truly imperative to clothe ourselves with compassion, kindness, humility, gentleness, and patience. With these qualities driving our thoughts and informing our will, we are certainly brought to a better place where we can actually forgive those who have wronged us.

Keep in mind, however, that while we extend forgiveness, we are not saying that bad behaviour or abuse is ever okay. It is not. Extending forgiveness is like trading really heavy boots for running shoes; it simply makes it easier to live the rest of today. Clearly the one who receives the forgiveness is also freed and can hopefully move forward. So often when dealing with our loved ones, repeatedly extending forgiveness won't make them stop their substance abuse. But it may be part of the solution.

My husband and I made many decisions based on our desire to have a relationship with our loved one when and if that day of sobriety came. So many addicts have burnt every bridge to the people who care for them. The day sadly comes when they find in their lives a void of anyone who truly loves them or is still in a relationship with them.

We wanted to be there to celebrate the day he would finally be finished with his drinking. I am very thankful for the choice we made to forgive repeatedly, even though it was never easy.

Dear Father,
Thank you for loving me. I confess to you that these character qualities are running thin where my loved one is concerned. I desperately need a fresh supply. Would you give this to me so I can love as I ought and forgive as you call me to?
In Jesus's name, amen.

HOW FORGIVENESS IMPROVES YOUR SITUATION
Day Five
Read Ephesians 4:29–32

Let no corrupting talk come out of your mouths… Let all bitterness and wrath and anger… be put away from you… Be kind to one another… forgiving one another, as God in Christ forgave you.
—Ephesians 4:29, 31–32

When I was growing up, my mom signed us kids up for bowling. I confess that I did not enjoy it. I did learn something, though. When you throw a bowling ball, you must watch the follow-through. The way you finish the throw is a big deal. The ball follows exactly where your arm and hand are pointed.

In today's passage, we are told to let no unwholesome word come out of our mouths. Negative talk reminds me of a bowling ball that will head straight to the gutter. The first words out of our mouths often determine how we manage whatever challenging situation we find ourselves in.

It's easy to despair when dealing with addictions or mental illness, as it can feel hopeless. When I heard that our loved one was out drinking again, the first words out of my mouth often determined the direction my thoughts would go. When I chose to say, "God, I cannot stop my son from drinking, but would you watch over his life right now?" what followed would be different. It brought hope into an otherwise hopeless situation, and it changed me, enabling me to extend grace and forgiveness.

Our text today tells us not only that we need to get rid of all bitterness and anger, but that we must extend compassion and forgiveness. The former is enough of a challenge, and we might think we have done our part by not holding onto anger and its many cousins.

Extending forgiveness and compassion is considerably further down the road. How will we ever do that? Our words can lead the way in this. It's not impossible. The words we speak out loud or in our hearts can determine which attitudes we will embrace today. The flavour of our words will not only benefit the recipient, but also the one who speaks them.

Dear Father,
As you have forgiven me, I choose to forgive my loved one. Help me today to say words that will heal and help. May my words reflect the hope I have in you. Forgive me for terrible words I have spoken that reflect a dark reality. I choose to dwell on a deeper reality, that you are at work right now in my loved one. Calm my fears and usher me into a new way of thinking today.
In Jesus's name, amen.

THE INDISPENSABLE PLACE OF THANKSGIVING
Week Three
Introduction

I have often heard it said that there is great power in giving thanks. It has become a daily practice over the years. The challenge, I find, is to give thanks to God when fear and sadness grip my heart.

I remember the many nights I would lay in my bed knowing that our son was out drinking somewhere. We had no idea where he was or when he would come home, or even if he would make it home safely. We knew he would be very drunk when he did make it home. Worry could consume my mind. I would listen for the door to open and for the footsteps on the stairs. At least I would know he was still alive. Only when I knew he was finally home would sleep come.

In the morning I would be exhausted, my heart weighed down with sadness. The thought of giving thanks to God, or even praising Him, honestly did not cross my mind.

Then I had an idea. It was simple, but in my humble opinion, brilliant. I started to practice giving thanks anyway, simply because I discovered the difference it made.

My routine was this: I would listen to the song "10,000 Reasons" by Matt Redman, usually a few times. Though I would have been feeling quite dead in my heart, soon, as I sang along, God's Holy Spirit would usher my heart and mind to a place where there was light and hope. I needed something doable and simple. This is what worked for me.

This week we will look at the value and practice of thanksgiving, even when life is messy.

A PATHWAY TO GOD'S PRESENCE
Day One
Read 1 Thessalonians 5:16–18

Rejoice always, pray without ceasing, give thanks in all circumstances; for this is the will of God in Christ Jesus for you.

—1 Thessalonians 5:16–18

We have a simple to-do list today:

1. Be joyful always.
2. Pray continually.
3. Give thanks in all circumstances.

Why these three things? Very simple: it is God's will. It's much easier to do this on a sunny day when life makes sense. It's much more difficult when things are confusing and our hearts struggle to make sense of what's happening.

Yet these words don't only apply to us when we're in a certain frame of mind. We are to give thanks all the time. Yet to be honest, I didn't feel joyful during that season of our son's frequent drinking bouts.

The trouble is that what we're facing seems so all-encompassing. Yet the reality is that God's love for us and the fact that we belong to him are more important truths than the sadness we are experiencing. There are varying degrees of truth, after all. What I'm describing is eternal truth, which therefore bears much greater weight. We are wise to dwell on that which is the deeper truth.

It is helpful to think of this list as a pathway to experiencing God in a deeper way. Turning intentionally to God with thanksgiving in our prayers brings us peace, for it reminds us that he is near us and so much greater than all that we face. The practice of thanksgiving leads us to joy because there is a change of focus. The situation doesn't appear as hopeless and dark. Our eyes suddenly look at a different centre. Giving thanks becomes a door opener; it leads us out of our despair and into the presence of God.

On the rough days, I love to picture the door to God's throne room. That door is never locked, and he is always waiting for me. As I give thanks, it's as though I walk through that door into his very presence, even though my circumstances haven't changed in the least.

Dear Father,
Thank you for the unchanging truths of your word. Thank you that I am your very own. I find security and safety in that knowledge. Thank you for hearing my prayer. I give thanks for your nearness and unfailing love. Thank you that your eye is upon my loved one even as it is upon me. Watch over my loved one. I thank you for my loved one.
In Jesus's name, amen.

A PATHWAY TO EXPERIENCING GOD'S PROMISES

Day Two

Read Psalm 28:6–7

Blessed be the Lord! For he has heard the voice of my pleas for mercy. The Lord is my strength and my shield; in him my heart trusts, and I am helped; my heart exults, and with my song I give thanks to him.

—Psalm 28:6–7

Years ago, I trudged twenty-two miles up a mountain on cross-country skis with a heavy backpack. After what seemed like hours of skiing up that winding path, finally the mountain shelter came into view and relief flooded over me.

God's mercy is like that. In this passage, the psalmist says that God's mercy brings great relief. There are many who don't understand what you're going through. Their comments reflect that. As a result, you are reluctant to be open with them.

God, however, understands completely. He knows your pain and deep anguish. You can call out to him knowing that he welcomes you. That brings relief—a deep sigh of the soul.

The fact that God hears our prayers and is attentive to our cries for mercy evokes thanksgiving in us. We know that we have God's ear. The knowledge that we are not alone makes our situation hopeful, for God hears us. Nothing is impossible to God, after all. If he hears us, we can be at rest, for he will take up our cause.

Because God hears us, we give thanks to him. This lends us confidence, whereas other things our loved one has done robs us of confidence. Perhaps things people have said to you have also robbed you of confidence, making you feel deeply alone. But God hears and does not condemn.

Don't miss this essential step: the giving of thanks. God's mercy to us is a fact, and it's in the giving of thanks that his promise takes root in us and changes our hearts. You will find the giving of thanks to be a real faith-builder if you're careful to actually do it. Joy will quietly slip into your heart and you will be ushered into a better attitude as you face your day.

Dear Father,
Thank you for your mercy and for hearing me when I call to you. Thank you for not condemning me though I feel my own inadequacies so deeply. Nothing is impossible with you, and this fills me with joy. Truly, I am not alone. Thank you for being my shield and strength today.
In Jesus's name, amen.

A KEY TO FINDING GOD'S PEACE

Day Three

Read Colossians 3:15–17

And let the peace of Christ rule in your hearts, to which indeed you were called in one body. And be thankful.
—Colossians 3:15

It is curious that the Bible says, *"Let the peace of Christ rule in your hearts."* The thought is that we must allow in the peace of Jesus, desirable as it is, if it is to rule. We are to let it rule. It wants to rule and is meant to do that. Though quiet, it is powerful and will transform you on any day you allow it to.

There are things we do, however, that either welcome the peace of Christ or keep it at bay.

Christ must rule in our hearts, and he brings peace with him. Peace accompanies his rule. If his peace is absent, it could well be that the poor decisions of your loved one are ruling you, or perhaps your fear of what they will do next. The first step is to move over and let him rule!

I've asked God, "What does this look like anyway?" I am a very practical person. As I sit and listen for his voice, I see two closets. One is full of confusion, broken promises, despair, and countless disappointments. The other is full of the truth we find in God's word: hope, the peace he gives, and his promises that encourage us.

Every morning, I stand peering into one of these closets. The question is simple. Where do I want to stand today? From which closet will I get dressed? When we choose the closet that is full of God's promises, we can take the proverbial "sweater" that is soaked in his peace and let it seep into our soul like rich lotion on very dry skin. It is a gift of his grace. Or we can choose the other. We have freedom. I choose peace.

Then we give thanks. That's how the peace of Christ is maintained in our hearts. Rather than fret, give thanks. Instead of thinking the worst, give thanks. In place of despair, give thanks. In this way, you let the peace of Christ continue to rule in your heart.

Dear Father,
Today I "put on" this peace that you promise me. Too long have I dressed myself with the garments of despair. I hereby acknowledge your gracious rule and give thanks to you. I trust you and yield to you. Your promises are life to me. I receive them with thanksgiving!
In Jesus's name, amen.

A MIGHTY SPIRITUAL WEAPON
Day Four
Read 2 Chronicles 20:21–22

"Give thanks to the Lord, for his steadfast love endures forever." And when they began to sing and praise, the Lord set an ambush… so that they were routed.

—2 Chronicles 20:21–22

As the story goes, the king in 2 Chronicles suddenly faced a massive enemy army; he was outmatched militarily, and the enemy was going to be upon him in only a day or two. The threat was real.

Though he had other options available to him, he chose to simply present himself and his people in a display of helpless dependence before the Lord. God responded with a definite word through the voice of a man with very specific instructions. The king recognized it as God speaking to him and put his faith in that word.

The next day, there was no second-guessing themselves. No one asked, "Did God really speak to us yesterday?" On the contrary, they organized themselves to go out to face the enemy, but their method was unusual. The king put the choir in front of the army and instructed the singers to give thanks to God.

Notice the correlation. As soon as they began singing songs of thanksgiving, God set an ambush against the enemy such that they were entirely defeated.

The lessons for us are clear. First, when we are overwhelmed by bad news that threatens to sink us, we are to become very quiet before God and wait for him. He speaks to us, usually in a still, small voice.

Second, thanksgiving is an expression of our confidence in God. Allow it to lead you. Your emotions will catch up. Don't wait for fear to dissipate. Thank him for the thing he has just spoken to your heart.

Third, the giving of thanks overcomes the enemy of our souls. Do you ever feel like there is another power, a dark thing, that has stepped into your loved one's life and drives them down a path of absolute destruction? It is an intimidating feeling. The giving of thanks is a mighty spiritual weapon that disarms that evil presence and drives away crippling darkness and hopelessness.

Dear Father,
Speak to me regarding this situation I face. My eyes are on you. Thank you for seeing me through my overwhelming situation. I put my faith in your word to me and give thanks. I delight to wield this mighty weapon as an expression of confidence in you. Deliver us from the evil that threatens. Bring us to a place of healing and peace.
In Jesus's name, amen.

A BEAUTIFUL OFFERING TO GOD
Day Five
Read Psalm 136

Give thanks to the Lord, for he is good, for his steadfast love endures forever.

—Psalm 136:1

Have you ever tried to take a picture but someone's head is in the way and frankly you can't see a thing? There are days when that is exactly how life feels. I would like to give thanks, or even feel God's love, but it's as if someone or something is standing in the way.

When I read this passage from Psalm 136, which presents a list of things the psalmist is giving thanks for and acknowledging each time that God's love endures forever, I am reminded that no event can occur that will supersede this important truth. While life may feel like shifting sand, this one truth does not move. His love endures forever.

Today is the only day we know we have. So let us make that choice today and be thankful for God's steadfast love. Begin your thanksgiving today with this one simple truth and let it inform every situation you presently face. Remember how he has been faithful to you specifically.

I attended a funeral once where a young man made a list of ten things he was thankful for. He did this from a posture of grief, for his mom had just died. He had prayed and believed God for healing and was very frustrated and disappointed in God. He recounted that from the time he had been a little boy, his mom had made him name ten things he was thankful for whenever he was frustrated or angry. He had discovered the power of thanksgiving at a young age, and it helped put things in perspective.

When life is hard, it's a struggle to remember that God has been faithful in days gone by. If you're having a difficult time with that, ask God to show you where he was in those most difficult moments. He has been with you all along and you must see that.

God is worthy of your thanksgiving because it means acknowledging what is true. He met you then and he will meet you again.

Dear Father,
Thank you for this new day. Thank you that your mercies are new every single morning. Thank you that your love endures forever and that it reaches out to me, as it does to my loved one. Thank you that there is no dark experience in our family that is greater than that fact. I rest in your love and commit my loved one to you.
In Jesus's name, amen.

FINDING COURAGE FOR COMPLICATED DECISIONS
Week Four
Introduction

I have never been in a position where I've had to make the decision to turn off a loved one's life support. I can only imagine how hard that would be, especially when it's your child.

As parents of an addict, or one with mental illness, we are often faced with the need to acknowledge that our help is not accomplishing what we hoped for anymore. To the contrary, we may be keeping them from becoming clean or sober. I remember well how I would pick up our loved one or make a nice meal or buy this or that all in the belief that it was going to be just the thing!

There came a time in our journey when we had to admit that providing room and board and everything else we were doing for our son was no longer helping him. Coming up with the courage to tell him we were not going to let him stay was one of the hardest conversations of our lives. Our fear was that we would lose our son, that our decision would create such a divide with him that the relationship would never recover. It was already so fragile.

The truth is, I was nearing a nervous breakdown. My husband could have hung on longer; I could not. The whole scene had become so unfruitful. Something had to change. For this change to happen, we would need help from God for sure!

Along this journey, courage is required on many different fronts. I would like to take the next five days to consider the encouragement that comes from God's word to make hard decisions.

CALLED TO COURAGE

Day One

Read Joshua 1:9

Have I not commanded you? Be strong and courageous. Do not be frightened, and do not be dismayed, for the Lord your God is with you wherever you go.

—Joshua 1:9

Over the years, we've all experienced seasons when we feel like shrinking violets on a windy day. Standing before us is a hard decision, one that will greatly impact the life of a loved one. A decision must be made—if only we possessed the courage.

It is natural to be reluctant to make any decision which could bring hardship or suffering to another. Though reluctant, we still need to do what's best for the one we love and for ourselves. Where do we go for that kind of courage? Frankly, the courage bank in my soul was often empty.

Courage is also needed when a line must be drawn. At what point has your loved one, within your own house, gone too far? To draw a line is very risky. Who knows what the reaction will be? We chose on one occasion to confiscate his wallet because we didn't want another night of drunkenness. He called the police on us. Would we do it again? Maybe. Is it right for one person to control the household through such ruinous behaviour?

The words found in today's reading remind us that we can be strong and courageous—not because we grit our teeth, but because of our knowledge that God is with us. Giving in to intimidation or fear isn't helpful. Passivity isn't a good decision in these cases. Parents are called to be courageous, not to just go with the flow.

Joshua was commanded to be courageous because of what God was calling him to do. Intimidation is not an option.

This journey is full of challenges. It's important to remember that we are not alone. God is with us. Consider: even if your decision isn't perfect, which in the world of addictions is quite likely, it's not the end of the world. God is able to make good from broken situations and imperfect decisions. Trust him. He is with you, as he is with the one you love.

Dear Father,
Life sometimes demands courage that I honestly don't have within myself. You promise that you are with me, and I can be strong and courageous. I ask that you help me today. I come with open hands, ready to receive. "I need thee every hour," like the old hymn says. Forgive me for my passivity. Help me be courageous. Give me all that I need for this day. Thank you, Lord.
In Jesus's name, amen.

HOW TO ACQUIRE COURAGE
Day Two
Read Isaiah 41:8–10

...fear not, for I am with you; be not dismayed, for I am your God; I will strengthen you, I will help you, I will uphold you with my righteous right hand.

—Isaiah 41:10

It's one thing to hear that we shouldn't be afraid on a windless, sunny day. It's quite another when the weather is stormy and the rain pounds against you. That is a fitting picture of what it's like to journey with an addict, or whatever's troubling your loved one. This verse then comes like a healing salve to an angry wound.

Isaiah was speaking to a people who felt very small. They were storm-tossed and felt that past mistakes had disqualified them from having a close relationship with God. They had little hope and felt more fear than anything. Yet God came tenderly to them and said, "Fear not."

God speaks to our fears. We need to hear him. How can we be courageous when gripped by fear? He speaks to our hearts such that his voice breathes life into us. His voice is not the same as any other voice. It's not merely a word of encouragement, as your neighbour might encourage you. His word brings strength and hope at times when we are indecisive and hopeless, helping us to lay our fears down at his feet. No longer are our fears crippling.

Courage then finds its source in God. It is so much more than positive thinking. He speaks to us personally and we are changed. Sometimes his voice is simply his peace, but it has the same effect. We know that we're not alone. We know we can make the next decision.

We have plenty of reasons to be fearful and anxious on this particular journey, but God here simply reminds us that we don't need to be because he is with us. He holds us safe in his hand. Zero instructions are required to look around anxiously; not looking around anxiously is a different experience. We must be intentional about that and base this new pattern in new practices, like listening to God and his unchanging character. Courage will follow. It may take some practice, but it's worthwhile even though it's hard.

Dear Father,
Thank you for your presence with me. Thank you that I can rest in your hand today. Let me hear your voice. Give me courage when I am fearful and passive. I ask that you deliver my loved one from evil today. I ask for your resting peace in my heart. I confess my great need of you today and every day.
In Jesus's name, amen.

HOW TO EXPLAIN COURAGE
Day Three
Read Philippians 4:12–13

I know how to be brought low, and I know how to abound. In any and every circumstance, I have learned the secret of facing plenty and hunger, abundance and need. I can do all things through him who strengthens me.
—Philippians 4:12–13

This journey we walk isn't for the faint in heart. It's a tough journey that requires the fine balance of doing what we can to wisely care for this loved one while having to make some heart-wrenching decisions along the way.

Our passage points out to us two things in particular. One is that we can learn how to be content in times of suffering as well as when things are good. Much as we want to run from these seasons of hardship, it is possible to find peace in them.

Second, we will learn that this is done through the power of Christ who strengthens us. There is no other source. There is no other way to explain the courage and confidence we need in order to function in a healthy way in the middle of the chaos of addictive or bizarre behaviour.

As I reflect on the agonizing decisions my husband and I have made concerning our son while in active substance addition, we looked beyond ourselves to God:

- when we had to be firm on something that displeased him.
- when trust became so diminished that we dared not leave our wallets or passwords lying around.
- when we were once again searching the back lanes and neighbourhood drinking establishments looking for him, so that he wouldn't be hurt in his great need.

Loving an addict will quickly deplete you of your resources. I've often heard people in this situation say, "You have to dig deep for the strength needed." For me, that pit was bone dry. I needed strength, courage, and wisdom that would come from a source outside of myself.

Today's Bible verse says, *"I can do all things through him who strengthens me."* This was and is how we have made it through difficult times. God has proved himself faithful over and over again. He does this for anyone who calls to him. That is the essence of courage.

Dear Father,
Thank you for your offer to me today that through you I can do all things. I confess that I am so tired and in deep need of your help. Please, strengthen me and give me courage for whatever I face today. Thank you for your constant presence. It is such a comfort to me.
In Jesus's name, amen.

HOW KNOWLEDGE BUILDS COURAGE
Day Four
Read Psalm 16

I have set the Lord always before me; because he is at my right hand, I shall not be shaken.

—Psalm 16:8

I remember the day our son phoned to say that he had taken an entire bottle of his prescription meds. He was despairing deeply in his heart over many things and wanted to dull the ache inside. My husband and I were a forty-five-minute drive away. We called an ambulance to pick him up and then drove to the hospital to meet him.

Looking back, I'm still surprised that I didn't completely freak out.

Knowledge is indeed a powerful thing. I know the one who holds our loved one's hand when we aren't there. I also know who stands near to me at the worst of times. I was relieved to just see our son at the hospital receiving good care, though I knew that the road to recovery would be a long one. The knowledge of God's loving and personal care gave me courage.

It's not unlike a child jumping into water to see their parent with their arms held out anticipating the big jump. The child courageously leaps with confidence, knowing that their parent will catch them.

Walking into the emergency ward that evening was like that. I sensed God's quiet presence. I had been through this whole thing before with my son. God met me then and I knew he would meet me again.

God didn't solve everything in an instant. Whether he solves things in a moment or over time, it's no less a miracle and no less divine. God gave me what I needed for that day. He was present to soothe my racing heart and quietly calm my fears.

God does this for us as he promises, but that doesn't mean it is easy. Courage doesn't mean an absence of fear. Rather, it means that fear doesn't disable us. That can be a moment by moment victory some days. The reason fear doesn't disable us is that our confidence is in God. The knowledge that God has our loved one in his hand, that he is near to us, is deeply calming.

Dear Father,
Thank you for your unwavering presence in my life. The knowledge of your love and keeping power is precious to me. That is my confidence today; it runs deeper than my fears. Because you are at my right hand, I will not be greatly shaken. Thank you for giving me the courage I need today. Watch over my loved one.
In Jesus's name, amen.

WHY COURAGE MATTERS
Day Five
Read 1 Samuel 17:17–54

And David said, "The Lord who delivered me from the paw of the lion and from the paw of the bear will deliver me from the hand of this Philistine."

—1 Samuel 17:37

I have always liked the story of David and Goliath. I love his mindset when he faced the giant. No one had to inform him of the grand size of the giant and his astonishing fighting reputation. Goliath's boastful taunting was intimidating to the entire army.

David, however, wasn't deterred at all. His confidence was in God. Courage filled his heart, and against all odds he overcame the giant. Goliath's towering stature was brought low, his boastful taunts silenced. Courage makes a big difference.

We understand this giant from a different point of view as we face the addict/mentally unwell loved one. It can feel like a giant has entered our homes and breathes intimidation over all who dwell there. This challenge towers over us. Its size is immense and threatening. It can fill our homes and affect every relationship. Furthermore, its taunts strike fear in our hearts. We feel small and helpless by comparison. If it weren't for the love we feel for the addict, we would run and hide, just like Israel's soldiers.

There is so much at stake. This is when courage makes the difference. We must stay and fight. Love keeps us there, doesn't it? We cannot yield to this giant. Giving in to his boastful taunts is unthinkable because love will not let our loved one go.

This giant is bigger than us, but it's not bigger than Christ. The fact that we are bound to Christ strengthens our hearts. His victory becomes ours. It takes courage to daily face this giant, but we live with hope. We do not stand alone. Our fight is always done in prayer and with the wisdom God gives us.

I pray that today you will find courage to stand firm on the boundaries you have set in this battle that faces you.

Dear Father,
We come to you today and stand against this giant called addiction. We ask in Jesus's name that you would intervene in my loved one's life. Bring the victory needed today. I pray that you would give me the courage that David had as he faced Goliath. Help me stand firm today and to know where to stand firm. In myself, I fall short of what is needed to face this giant. Help me, Father.
In Jesus's name, amen.

OVERCOMING NUMBNESS
Week Five
Introduction

Many of us have faced the familiar feeling of going completely numb. When sorrow and stress leaves you this overwhelmed, numbness is often the result. The question we face is this: how do we get out of this mud puddle of numbed feelings?

I remember well the last summer during which our son drank. I was exhausted beyond words. It was the beginning of summer and I was at a Christian camp by myself. They had a speaker every day, and I chose to go and try to listen.

As I sat in the meeting, the teaching was passing me by. I have a memory of the speaker asking, "What can you do for God today?" Let's see… I couldn't think of anything I could do for him. On the other hand, there were a number of things I would have loved for him to do for me. I needed a fresh wind to blow through my weary soul. I needed a fresh dose of hope and peace. I needed to be reminded that God was paying attention to what we were living through. I needed him to renew me from the depths of my being.

I didn't know where to start.

Have you ever felt like this? I sat in the sunshine at that camp and got out my Bible and journal. I began to write out Bible verses, verses of hope and promise.

When I began my project, I felt nothing. I was just writing and hoping to put some new thoughts in my head. Slowly, God, through the power of his word, breathed life into me. It was like a gentle breeze blowing through my soul.

We want to take a few days this week to reflect on some verses that will, we pray, have that same life-giving effect on anyone who cares to listen. Perhaps you too wish to write the verses out in a journal.

THE DANGERS OF FORGETTING
Day One
Psalm 103:1–5

...forget not all his benefits...

—Psalm 103:2

I love baking, and I'm pretty good at it. I would say it's my happy place. I'm not open-a-bakery-tomorrow good at it, but I can bake great cookies, muffins, and loaves. All this baking is wonderful, except for when I have to do it and feel anxious over what's going on around me. That is when I forget whether I added the salt or how many cups of flour... This is a big deal in baking!

In this psalm, we are told not to forget all of God's benefits. To forget his benefits is essentially the same as forgetting him. And to forget God is to be banished to our circumstances. That's when we lose heart and sometimes act rashly. We jump to conclusions, saying things we regret. Faith dissipates and despair takes its place.

Scripture speaks many times of the dangers of forgetting God. We feel alone and begin acting as if we are alone. That's a dark path and one that comes to us far too easily.

Faith, however, is strengthened by active memory. If we don't want to forget his benefits, we must intentionally remember them. For example, remembering that God forgives all our sin is enough to make our souls sing. In addition, he is our healer, for both body and soul. It is not an overstatement to say that he has crowned us with his love and satisfies us with so much good that the vigour of youth returns to us.

None of these are overstatements, as if we might be guilty of overselling what God truly does! He fills each of these statements with his presence as we call them to mind. These reminders make our souls sing even when our circumstances haven't changed.

Today, if you desire to experience a fresh wind of God blowing through your weary soul, take time to write out Psalm 103. As you write each verse, take a moment to thank him. Live in that verse and don't rush past it. Let the fresh breeze begin!

Dear Father,
I choose to bring to my memory the great things you have done for me. Forgive me for forgetting so easily. I have lost sight of you. Thank you for your word that draws me back. I ask that you bring a fresh wind of life into me today. Thank you for your unfailing love. Heal my soul today, as your word says. Thank you.
In Jesus's name, amen.

BREATHE IN GOD'S WORD
Day Two
Isaiah 55:6–11

...so shall my word be that goes out from my mouth; it shall not return to me empty, but it shall accomplish that which I purpose, and shall succeed in the thing for which I sent it.

—Isaiah 55:11

When I go to the cosmetic area of the drugstore and look for some kind of facial cream that promises to "diminish fine lines," I would love to find one that actually does so for more than one hour. Though undoubtedly it helps, these creams have some major limitations regardless of what they claim.

God's promises are different. Consistently, God speaks things before they are and then works to accomplish them. Once his word goes out, he brings all kinds of factors into play by his own power. Whether a circumstance is hopeful matters little, because God is at work. Nothing is impossible to him. Even if there seems to be no way through this dilemma you find yourself in, continue to hold on to the word of God and live in his promises. He doesn't need an open path: he simply creates it.

There is so much hope for us in this. First, we know that God has a good purpose in mind for all that he says to us. Second, he has the power to accomplish those purposes for us regardless of the circumstances. Third, his word is always doing something in us, as we read it, hear it, meditate on it, or write it out.

One of the ways in which God brings a fresh wind to our soul is through his word. We drift from it to our peril. I remember the exhaustion I felt as I sat down to write out his word. I needed him to bring forward the purposes of his heart for me and he did it, though I was totally numb at the time. I didn't have to hold my breath or hang from my toes; he just did what he said he would.

I have always found Jesus to be the Gentle Shepherd. He gently addresses the lies and bad attitudes I store up in my heart. He ministers to our hearts through his word, breathing life, hope, and encouragement.

Dear Father,
Thank you for your word. As I meditate on it, you quietly accomplish your purposes. Thank you for your good purposes. I humbly receive your word. Forgive me for drifting from it. I welcome heaven's thoughts and attitudes. Breathe life into my soul. Thank you for hearing my prayers and being so present with me.
In Jesus's name, amen.

FRESH PATHWAYS TO THE HEART
Day Three
Read Psalm 119:25–32

My soul clings to the dust; give me life according to your word... teach me your statutes! Make me understand the way of your precepts... My soul melts away for sorrow; strengthen me according to your word!
—Psalm 119:25–28

Years ago, I went backpacking in the mountains. It was winter and the group I was with had to carry heavy backpacks and wear cross-country skis. If we were careful to keep the weight of that backpack perfectly centred and not waver to the left or right, we were fine.

However, if we lost our balance even slightly, we would fall with the backpack, often pressing our faces into the snow. Getting up again was difficult. The long trip up the mountain wasn't the tiring part; it was falling and struggling to get up again.

Many of us can relate to the image this passage opens with, being laid low in the dust. As we consider the state of our lives as we walk with a loved one who's struggling, not only are they laid low in the dust, we are often covered in the dust ourselves. It is not the dust alone that is so troublesome; it is the weariness that fills us to the brim.

What surprises us is the outcome. If we begin at the low point, clinging to the dust, our souls nearly spent, how do we end up full of life? Life comes to us through the word of God.

The same is repeated later in our text. This time the beginning image is of a soul full of sorrow; the endpoint is a position of strength. And the means once again is the word of God.

Writing out God's word in this season gave me something else to think about. It drew my mind down a different path, a much more wholesome path: God's path. Meditating on God's word reprograms our thought patterns. Instead of thinking about how messed up our loved ones' lives are and the gripping fear of where it's all headed, we are led by God's word into thoughts that fill us with life and strength. God dwells in those thoughts and will refresh you with the wind of his presence.

Dear Father,
Thank you for your willingness to bend low and pick me up from the dust, the mess I find myself in today. Strengthen me according to your word. Breathe hope and encouragement into me today as I meditate on your word. I want to come into alignment with your thoughts. In Jesus's name, amen.

GOD'S GOT IT IN HAND
Day Four
Read 1 Peter 5:6–11

And after you have suffered a little while, the God of all grace, who has called you to his eternal glory in Christ, will himself restore, confirm, strengthen, and establish you.

—1 Peter 5:10

There is a restaurant in my town that adds to each meal a package of my favourite chocolates. I don't eat them often, but I do love them. When I eat these chocolates after months of not eating them, I remember just how wonderful they taste. I eat one and savour it.

That summer as I sat in my place of exhaustion, I had forgotten many of the wonderful truths that are found in Scripture. I had been so overwhelmed with sorrow. I was emotionally drained.

God's got it all in hand: that's what I see here. This is the prized chocolate. First, the best stance for us to take right now is to humble ourselves before him so that he lifts us up. Humility always invites God. Do all you can to remove roadblocks, like pride, as they block the way to him.

Second, since he cares for you, cast your anxieties onto him. He's all ears concerning your plight.

Third, since he is infinitely greater than the devil, who is presently causing such wreckage in your family, resist the devil—for you are in Christ. This is no longer to be the devil's playground.

Fourth, though you feel alone in your suffering, you are not. There are many who face the same battle. Find other people of faith who share your struggle and join with them in prayer. This is part of God's provision for you.

Finally, without predicting outcomes, God says that this storm won't last forever. No storm does. After it's done, he himself will restore and strengthen you.

Though you feel dead inside, hold to the hope that God is greater than this whole grievous situation you find yourself in. He has both you and this situation in hand. Look to him. That strong hope in God comes like a fresh breeze to your soul. He will satisfy you in what seems to be a sun-scorched land.

Dear Father,
Thank you for having it all in hand, as you do me. You are greater than all: I need not fear. I humble myself before you and confess every prideful way. Lead me to a good friend who shares this same journey. I also take my stand against the evil one in this situation and oppose him because I belong to you. My loved one belongs to you. Fulfill your promises in my loved one and restore me.
In Jesus's name, amen.

GOD AND GOD ALONE
Day Five
Read Psalm 62

For God alone my soul waits in silence; from him comes my salvation.

—Psalm 62:1

It was a bright and sunny summer day when I walked to a quiet place at our campground. There was water, trees, and lots of birds. I dragged myself into a chair and took out my Bible and journal. My soul was weary, but I was thankful for this little hideaway. I made the most of it. I was continuing in my habit of writing down one scripture after another.

Today I came to Psalm 62.

Like David, you probably feel yourself to be in a place of confinement, a place not of your choosing. In addition, you may feel alone. It could be that others have made you feel small, since no such burden should fall upon a God-fearing household. Like the psalmist, you have been made to feel the assaults of those whose words have had the effect of thrusting you down and crushing you. You looked for compassion but were hurt by those you trusted. As a result, you have isolated yourself, perhaps for the sake of your survival. To make matters worse, the words of your loved one have at times come like daggers into your soul, further isolating you and making you feel a failure.

That is Psalm 62. One of the keys here is to see your place of confinement differently. The fortress you find yourself in, and which others have in a certain sense created, becomes the very place in which you meet God. Though others have pushed you there, it becomes a place of closeness with God where he reveals himself to you and fills you up. He then becomes a safe place, a refuge for your soul. Where others have disappointed you, God has proved faithful.

In the end, people do disappoint, though not all. The key is to find those who are faithful friends. God, however, is always faithful. He and he alone is our source, our strength. When you find God to be your strength in that place of confinement, you will not be shaken.

I remember how our family used to camp deep in the woods when our kids were small. All the kids wanted to be in the tent where their dad was. They felt safer knowing he was there. Such is the confidence of the person who has placed their trust in God and God alone.

Dear Jesus,
Thank you for being my refuge and strength, right in this place of confinement. How gracious you are. I forgive those who have hurt and disappointed me. I forgive my loved one too. My trust is in you only. Refresh me here through your word.
In Jesus's name, amen.

FINDING HOPE IN THE DITCH OF DESPAIR

Week Six

Introduction

As the day wore on, the knot in my stomach grew. It had been a few days since our son had been drinking and I knew it would start again. Sure enough, the text would come or the deafening silence. I knew he was out drinking, and the feeling of hopelessness would flood my heart.

When will this end, Lord? I prayed. *How much longer must we endure this?*

I would work at getting through my day as I knew I could do nothing to stop the drinking or shorten the binge. No matter what I did. But he was constantly on my mind, and it was hard to think about anything else. I remember being in business meetings or having people over and struggling to be present. It was never easy. I would pray and thank God that he could see our son when I couldn't.

I also had a few pieces of literature from Al Anon that I would read. I found that it brought me some hope from those who knew this journey all too well.

I remember how I wished I could simply send him a nice text begging to come home. Then he would text me back saying, "Oh right, Mom. I should not do this again. I will be home in ten minutes." Then he would walk in the door. Wouldn't that be nice?

Unfortunately, it doesn't work like that. Trust me. I tried.

Feelings of hopelessness are common in families dealing with addictions and mental illness. This is due in part to feeling so powerless. Also, the fact that this painful journey has no sure end date tends to fill people with despair.

God's word was and continues to be a source of hope for us. Our readings this week will unpack this important theme. Our prayer is that you will find yourself in a better place emotionally at the end of it.

THE ANATOMY OF HOPE

Day One

Read Romans 12:12

Rejoice in hope, be patient in tribulation, be constant in prayer.

—Romans 12:12

How does one put on joy in hope while standing in the middle of a storm that seems to have no end? I like to think of this passage as a circle, one thing leading to the other and on to the next until we're back at the beginning where we start over again.

Hope comes in various sizes. It can fill a room or hang by a thread. This is a reference to hope that is so sure that it fills you with joy. It's a confidence that is full of certainty. Such hope can never be based on the promise of an addict. It's anchored in the unchanging character of God who hears your prayers and is present to your loved one in a way that, even at this moment, you never can be.

Hope is not a denial of difficulty. It looks trials straight in the eye and doesn't flinch. Denial is strong among addicts, but not with people of hope. Hope sees things for what they are. You can live with a great deal of adversity and still be full of hope.

The next step in the Romans 12:12 triad is to be patient in tribulation. The way out of addiction is generally a long road, and patience is evidence of hope. We are waiting for God, not our loved one; our hope is in him. Similar truths apply to those with mental illness.

Neither is prayer inconsistent with hope. Hope manifests in prayer and is not passive. Prayer acknowledges the living partnership we have with God, for he hears us and acts. Some things he has simply determined not to do unless we pray. We pray because we feel a promise in our heart from God for a loved one. It is hope that drives us to prayer.

Dear Father,
You are the God of all hope. Give me a promise for my loved one that I can hold onto. Also, show me where you are in this situation so I can be full of hope. I must see beyond what my eyes can grasp. Strengthen my heart with hope. What is the next thing you are doing in my loved one? I wait for you to guide me in how to pray. My eyes are on you. Even now, you fill me with joy in your presence.
In Jesus's name, amen.

FOCUS ON THE LONG GAME
Day Two
Read Psalm 30

Weeping may tarry for the night, but joy comes with the morning.

—Psalm 30:5

Suffering can feel eternal. One day I had to go see my doctor, as I had been unwell for several months. The doctor said to me, "Donna, I know that what you are going through right now feels like forever, but it will pass." And it did.

Psalm 30 reminds us that suffering has an expiry date, even if we cannot see it. The viewpoint of the psalmist is the long game. He looks over many years and knows that one day all will be made right, and in this he finds hope. Therefore, he can sing and give thanks to God.

There are things that can help us not lose hope in the long game. First, remember how God has drawn you out of dark places (Psalm 30:1–3). Others sank down in the deep waters, but God drew you out of all that, though it didn't happen overnight.

Second, while there are seasons during which God's displeasure seems obvious and confusion seems to reign, that is not the norm (Psalm 30:4–5). Rather, his favour lasts a lifetime for all who look to him.

Third, God will show his favour to you (Psalm 30:6–7). This remains true while we feel our dependence upon him, for whoever trusts in him will know his good favour. God takes time to build the things he does, both in us and our loved ones.

Fourth, though it seems your life is ebbing away and your plight is desperate, God's highest praise comes from those very ones whom he has delivered from such a dark place (Psalm 30:8–12).

Anyone journeying through the valley of addiction with a loved one must keep the long game in mind, no matter how bleak it looks. Looking to God for what lies ahead ushers in hope and a better perspective than feeling stuck in the realities of the present day.

There is a saying that tells, "Perspective is everything." We still must deal with the challenges of today, but we can have hope that there is indeed a future that looks quite different than this moment in which we find ourselves.

Dear Father,
Perhaps the most pressing thing coming out of this reading is the reminder that I have perhaps failed my loved one, and I sometimes sense your divine displeasure. Forgive me of any shortcomings I have brought into this difficult situation. My own mistakes rob me of hope. Show me your favour. Thank you for your promise that favour lasts a lifetime. I want to live in that promise. Renew hope in me. Thank you for your mercy.
In Jesus's name, amen.

THE SOURCE OF HOPE
Day Three
Read Romans 15:13

May the God of hope fill you with all joy and peace in believing, so that by the power of the Holy Spirit you may abound in hope.

—Romans 15:13

How do we know when we are experiencing hope that comes from God himself? It is, first, a heart full of joy and peace; second, hope itself will be in such abundance that only God could produce it, given the circumstances. Both the nature and measure of what is produced makes us conclude that the result was accomplished unquestionably by God.

Did you notice that God's title here is "God of hope"? Hope describes him. It is essential to his character. In addition, hope is what he produces in us. Hope is birthed in us by his presence in our lives. It is by the power of the Holy Spirit that we come to a place of hope. It becomes a miracle. It is a function of God's working in us. It doesn't rise naturally within us, not even among those who are optimists by nature. Even they, when pushed to an extreme place, can be brought low and despondent. Hope is not a function of personality. God is the author of hope; it comes by his power.

The way to make hope real in your present situation is to trust him, to simply believe that he rewards you as you seek him and is attentive to your prayers. Even more specifically, the practice of thanking him brings it all together.

When fear or sorrow threatens, as it often does, I choose to combat those thoughts by saying, "Thank you, God, for caring for my loved one. Thank you for hearing my prayers today. Thank you for giving what is needed." Through practicing this intentionally, God's peace and joy have crept beautifully into my heart. You may not get there all at once, and it may come incrementally as other things are dealt with in our hearts, and I assure you that God means to supply you with a bounty of hope. That's the direction in which God means to take you. Hope finds its source in him; trust him.

Dear Father,
Thank you for being present to me. You are infinitely greater than the situation I find myself in with my loved one. I look to you and thank you. Help me to remember all that I can thank you for in my present situation. Fill me with hope through the power of the Holy Spirit. I acknowledge that I am not, of myself, a source of hope; only you are. Thank you.
In Jesus's name, amen.

THE ESSENCE OF HOPE
Day Four
Read 1 Chronicles 16:8–13

Seek the Lord and his strength; seek his presence continually!

—1 Chronicles 16:11

When I had the first inkling that my loved one was out drinking again, my wisest response was to look to God immediately. My simple prayer would go like this: "Here we go again, God. Please help him and help me." Prayers never need to be complicated. They need to be sincere and full of faith.

Such a prayer would be the first of many as the long hours went by. I would seek God to watch over my son when I knew he was incapable of doing so himself. I would talk to God throughout the day as I did simple things like make a meal or complete tasks for work. I would invite him to help me. Hardly a minute would go by when my husband and I weren't lifting our son up to God in prayer. Whatever else we were doing, our minds were with him, and our hearts were looking up to God to intervene.

This would go on throughout an entire day until late evening when Bill would go out to hopefully find our boy, bring him home, and pray him free of the evil spirits that had become attached to him through the things he had done.

Was it easy? Never. We were intentional in our prayers. Seeking God for the simplest of things made a great difference to me. As we seek God continually, regardless of our circumstances, we find hope where there was previously little to none.

As we seek God and read his word, we discover insights which lead to hope we can rest in. During such trying days, God speaks specific and definite words to our hearts that fill us with hope while giving us direction in how next to pray. He can guide us where there is no clear path, offering us specific words of promise and direction. How else can we navigate these difficult paths where we have never been before? God will do this for us as we intentionally and continually seek him.

Dear Father,
Today I will be found seeking you first, foremost, and continually. Before I tell everyone about the trials of today or the choices of my loved one, I choose to seek you. I pray that you would quiet my heart today with your love. Give me a word regarding my loved one. How next would you have me to pray? What is the next thing you are going to do? I find my rest in you.
In Jesus's name, amen.

THE STRENGTH OF HOPE
Day Five
Read Psalm 46

God is our refuge and strength, a very present help in trouble… Be still, and know that I am God.
—Psalm 46:1, 10

I grew up not far from a line of bluffs along the shores of Lake Ontario. Every year people have fought to arrest the persistent erosion here. The lake's waves, coupled with wind, are a tough opponent. People whose backyards bump up against these bluffs know that each year their property will get a little bit smaller.

When I read Psalm 46, I am reminded of the passing of my father, who was also an alcoholic. He never really achieved sobriety, though I am told he cut back his drinking significantly in the last year of his life.

I was away in another province attending college when he died suddenly. While flying back to attend his funeral, I read this psalm. I thought about my life with my father over many years. As much as I loved my dad and wept at the thought of his passing and not being able to say goodbye in person, I was also acutely aware of the suffering he had caused to those who loved him.

I remember feeling like I was living this psalm in the years of dealing with my dad, then my brother, and finally my son, all struggling with substance addictions. It reminds us that though it feels like our lives are slowly being eroded by waters that *"roar and foam"* (Psalm 46:3), that the earth under us seems to be giving way (Psalm 46:2), we need not fear for God is with us (Psalm 46:5). This means we can function and go on living even while the waves hammer at us. It also means that we never stop looking to God for a serious breakthrough in the lives of our loved ones. Hope is strong in trouble.

Be still then and know that God is still God. Maybe being still is actually the biggest challenge. It has certainly been mine. Remember, you don't have to fix your loved one, nor can you. Stop everything and wait on God. What does he say to you? He is with you.

Dear Father,
Thank you for your gracious presence with me in the storm. I quiet myself before you. Forgive me for taking upon myself that which only you can do, all the while failing to do what you actually call me to do. Enable me to keep on with the rest of my life, for this storm is not the centre. And deliver my loved one from this terrible peril. Sustain me with your peace.
In Jesus's name, amen.

SEEING BEYOND THE BROKENNESS

Week Seven

Introduction

The worst phone calls I have ever received were the ones when I heard my son's voice while he was in hospital following a suicide attempt. There are no words to describe the despair that grips one's heart at such a time.

In our church work, we have performed funerals for many who have taken their own lives. We have also steered many away from that outcome. Life near the streets is full of untimely death. We never thought, however, that it would come into our own house.

This week will focus on finding the peace of God during unimaginable fear and sorrow. Perhaps you, dear reader, have lost a loved one to suicide or an untimely death. May God comfort you and give you his peace.

God's mercy is new every morning. This is a reminder to us that each day there are new possibilities for our loved ones, just as there are for us.

Only God has the power to give us peace during these times as we sit in emergency rooms and endure long stays in psychiatric wards. Only God can calm the fear that chokes us. Only God can restore the life of those whom we love so much.

It's one thing to love the child who is excited to live another day, and quite another when despair so grips their heart and clouded mind that they believe death to be the only way to find relief.

May God meet you each day this week as we look at passages that we trust will bring us different perspectives and hope for another day. This is a one-day-at-a-time journey. Frankly, that is all anyone can manage most days.

A DESPERATE PEACE
Day One
Psalm 4

In peace I will both lie down and sleep; for you alone, O Lord, make me dwell in safety.

—Psalm 4:8

There are many people we might call when we receive word that our loved one is in the emergency ward after trying to take their own life. In Psalm 4, the psalmist makes only one call—and that is to God himself. He calls out of his distress and begs for mercy, simply that God would hear his desperate prayers.

Prayers become very focused at this point: "God, have mercy on my loved one! Bring peace to their troubled mind and sort out the mess that is filling them!" It is a pleading prayer and so desperate.

Your mind races. What has brought them to this point? How is it that death, in their mind, could be the only reasonable option? There's a bit of anger too. Who opened this door for them into the cavernous world of death? You, of course, see a thousand great things about their life and advantages they have—but not one of them matters at this moment to your loved one. They are in a place of great despair.

Yet God is near to the broken-hearted. He gives us relief in our distress, declares the psalmist. Desperate prayers usher in a desperate peace. It's quite unexplainable how God's peace comes underneath such sorrow and makes it manageable.

I needed him to sit in the chair on the other side of the bed and tell me there is a new day coming. As I prayed and sat through several long days in various hospitals, I found peace. Was it constant? No, I had to go back to the author of peace and seek his face again. It is hard to keep your focus on God while sitting next to one who is filled with utter despair. Where else can we go but to God himself?

Dear Father,
How did we get to this point? Have mercy on my loved one. Bring peace to their troubled mind. Open their eyes to see what they do not see. Deliver them from death and bind the spirit of death who whispers urgently in their ear. I place my trust in you, God, to do what no doctor can do. Though I see little change in my circumstances, I am not without hope. Thank you for your peace. Thank you for the strength you give to me hour by hour.
In Jesus's name, amen.

POINTED PRAYERS

Day Two
Read Psalm 5

Give attention to the sound of my cry, my King and my God, for to you do I pray. O Lord, in the morning you hear my voice; in the morning I prepare a sacrifice for you and watch.

—Psalm 5:2–3

No matter how dark the backdrop, God answers prayer. We sometimes become territorial, thinking that certain places and difficulties are beyond his reach. Certainly, sitting in psych wards with a loved one who would rather be dead than alive, hearing the high security metal doors clank shut, will test your faith. If you've ever had doubts about the effectiveness of prayer, those thoughts will come into full maturity at such a time.

Nothing, though, could be further from the truth.

The psalmist reminds us that we can lay our burdens before God in prayer as soon as we wake up, then wait in expectation for his answers. God is personal and invites personal conversation as we lay out our definite requests before him.

Prayer is a desperate cry. God isn't particularly taken by fancy words, though he notices urgency just like a parent does and pays attention. Also, this prayer is specific. There is no such thing as a general cry. The prayer is borne out of definite need. The greater the desperation, the more specific the prayer becomes; it's inevitable.

Finally, the prayer is given up with expectation that help will come in such a way that brings definite relief.

I have stood amazed at the specific answers to prayer that have come to us at precisely those occasions when all seems bleak. Darkness, though, is as light to God; he inhabits all of it. He sent people, brought help, met our boy right there, kept him safe, and moved him on to the next stone on the pathway towards restoration.

That's where prayers become so specific. What is the next thing, the next step towards wholeness? Ask God for that and you too will begin to see many more answers to your prayers.

Dear Father,
Thank you for not disregarding my prayers but being eager to hear and answer. Lord, show me what is the next thing you would have me ask you for regarding my loved one. Thank you for inhabiting dark and hopeless places with your presence. Give me eyes to see you in the dark.
In Jesus's name, amen.

DETERMINED TO LIVE
Day Three
Read Psalm 118

I shall not die, but I shall live, and recount the deeds of the Lord.

—Psalm 118:17

I cannot count how many times I told my husband, "This journey with our son is killing me." I felt like a part of my heart would die every single time I found out he was in the hospital again.

Near the middle of Psalm 118 are these words: *"I shall not die, but I shall live, and recount the deeds of the Lord"* (Psalm 118:17). To live becomes a choice, both for you and definitely your loved one. Once that doorway to death has been opened, to live is often a daily choice for your loved one. Pray this verse for them until they are determined to live and are themselves recounting what God has done for them.

You may have to guard your own heart too. In such chaotic and heart-breaking times, when the climb seems so steep, you will wonder how you can keep going. You sit there in hospital with your loved one hour after hour, surrounded by the quiet because they don't want to talk, or maybe because there's nothing to say. Where will you live in your thoughts?

Consider this to be your main thought right now: the steadfast love of the Lord endures forever. Now you are on solid ground.

One more thing: be careful regarding self-deprecation. As we read in Psalm 118:18, *"The Lord has disciplined me severely..."* At such times, we easily blame ourselves and see this as the discipline of God. And if we don't say that, others may.

God does discipline us, unquestionably. And no doubt we have not been perfect in our care for our loved one, so there's lots of room for blame. However, the focus of Scripture is on God who delivers us from death, not pushing us towards it. Even here, the psalmist says, *"but he has not given me over to death"* (Psalm 118:18). Turn away from those thoughts and remember today's verse: *"I shall not die, but I shall live, and recount the deeds of the Lord."* Live there.

Dear Father,
Thank you for your great love, which reaches out to me in this very place. Forgive me for every way in which I have contributed to this dark situation. Have mercy on me and my loved one. We choose life and turn away from death. Remove every thought of the desirability of death over life. The benefits of the death of your son enable us to live. We want to live and see the great things you will do in our lives. Give me wisdom in every conversation now.
In Jesus's name, amen.

A FAVOURABLE OUTCOME
Day Four
Read Romans 8:28–39

And we know that for those who love God all things work together for good, for those who are called according to his purpose.

—Romans 8:28

When we're in the middle of a crisis, it seems a bit of a stretch to think that anything good could come of it. The entire picture seems to be something of an enemy to us. Yet we look for hope and the assurance that, coming out the other end of this trial, we will be brought to something beautiful and altogether good. It's all rooted in the character and ability of God.

First, we believe that God is active in every circumstance of our lives, even those we weren't remotely looking for. Yet here we are, in a nightmare. Regardless, God is with us, bringing something good of it. He works for our good in *all* circumstances.

Second, we believe that he can work in the middle of messy situations that seem completely out of control. Sitting in hospital rooms with a loved one who is listless, among other things, is a strong reminder that we have little control over what's happening. Yet the promise holds true. It is not dependent upon what our eyes see in the moment, thankfully!

Third, it's completely beyond our reach to think of what good could possibly come of this trial when we're in the middle of it. Unless God gives us a picture of what this will look like at the other end, we really have no idea and can only walk humbly before him, praying and trusting. Looking back, once you're through it, is different. Then you can see much that is praiseworthy.

When I was a child, I was once asked by a teacher to draw a certain picture. I thought mine looked terrible. The teacher, who was an excellent artist, asked if she could help me. She drew just a few lines on my messy picture, and suddenly my drawing made better sense.

God is a bit like this. What we see is disorder. Staring at it only feeds the despair and fear in our hearts. Yet God is at work through it all, making something beautiful. In that, we find peace.

Dear Father,
Thank you that I am bound to you, and you to me through Christ. Thank you that you are the purposeful redeemer. I yield to you both the circumstances and my limited perspective and trust you with them. May your purposes go forward. Somehow you will bring forth beauty from ashes.
In Jesus's name, amen.

KEEP MOVING
Day Five
Read Psalm 23

Even though I walk through the valley of the shadow of death, I will fear no evil, for you are with me; your rod and your staff, they comfort me.

—Psalm 23:4

Have you ever walked in a forest on a cloudy night when you can't see the hand in front of your face? That is not our path, though it may seem like it. We don't walk through the pitch-black valley of death. Rather, we walk through the valley of the shadow of death.

I would much rather deal with the shadow of death than death itself. The shadow only passes over us. We feel its coolness as it temporarily steals the light, but a shadow doesn't really have substance. It points to a larger reality that does have substance, but that is not our portion, even though it is near to us, threatening us. Although we may feel its presence, its boast is too large; all that comes to us is its shadow. Why? Because God is with us, the very light of the world. When he is there, darkness cannot rule the day.

Something else: did you notice that we don't stand in this valley? Rather, we walk through it. We aren't stuck there. This is not our new address. We don't even pitch a tent. There is definite movement to our time in the valley of the shadow of death. Though it is unfamiliar territory to us, there is one who guides us through. That's why we don't get stuck. The Good Shepherd walks with us. He has in his hand both rod and staff. With one he pushes us along, and with the other he pulls us back from dangerous places we ought not to be.

It is noteworthy that evil is present in this valley. We feel its eerie presence. It seems unfair that it would take advantage of our vulnerability, but we need not fear because, again, God is with us. Evil is no match for him. It is a great comfort to be bound to him and kept by him in the valley of the shadow of death. Here we find peace.

Dear Father,
Thank you for your presence in the valley of the shadow of death. You are with me in what would otherwise be a terrifying reality. Manifest your presence to me. Make me know your comfort more than all these dark realities that fill my senses. Deliver me from all evil and keep me from stumbling. Thank you for your peace.
In Jesus's name, amen.

THE EVER-PRESENT PROMISES OF GOD
Week Eight
Introduction

Despair is sadly a common theme that most people struggle with when walking with a loved one caught up in addiction. I was certainly in that camp. I found the mountain of disappointments, lies, and fear that trudged alongside us to be exhausting.

One night I sat in my living room, marinating in a fresh dose of despair after a largely sleepless night, one that was marked again by our son's drinking. After growing sick of all my negative thoughts, I turned to my heavenly Father and prayed. The thought that came to me was this: all of God's promises are still true, for me and for our son. Many reading this wonder why I would ever believe otherwise.

I am orthodox in my beliefs. What catches us by surprise, though, is how deeply wearing this journey is on a person. The road is neither easy nor short. Perhaps it's a little like watching a loved one waste away with a terminal illness, except that in this case it is addiction, and with addiction is attached shame, disappointment, and anger. Watching someone you love choose to walk out the door with the full knowledge that they are going to fall deeper into the depth of the pit is gut-wrenching. As it must be horrible for the one living it, so it is for those watching. It is exhausting and frustrating. In such cases, it's not hard to lose sight of God's promises. This was certainly true for me.

This week we will consider a few promises we can hold on to and be thankful for. This is always life-giving for us.

THE UNFAILING PRESENCE OF GOD

Day One

Read Psalm 9:9–10

And those who know your name put their trust in you, for you, O Lord, have not forsaken those who seek you.

—Psalm 9:10

When I was growing up, we always had a cat. I loved our cat, as did my brother and sister. For us, the cat was more faithful to us than people were. My dad drank, my parents fought, and we were terrified. My cat would lick my tears when I cried. She was my comfort. I didn't know God at that point, so the cat was the best I could get.

What a comfort that God will *never* forsake me. It sounds so basic. Yet, to be honest, our practice deviates somewhat from our beliefs at times like this. We can tell by the level of anxiety and fear that grips our hearts.

In addition, it's not uncommon for friends to distance themselves from you when you go through rough waters. They probably still love you but are at a loss as what to do or say regarding your suffering. So they do nothing and sometimes withdraw. It makes you reluctant to speak openly of your challenges. It's a compounding reality that can make one feel alone. To make matters worse, it's not an affliction that goes away after two or three weeks. The good news is that God's not like people.

It seems to me that the greatest truths are the ones we keep coming back to. They always deserve deeper application in our lives. It's not that we have forgotten them. Rather, when we find ourselves in a new and challenging situation where we've suddenly lost our footing, that same familiar truth needs to be freshly applied.

Perhaps it catches us a bit by surprise that God is with us even in such a dark place. He has not forsaken you. There's no road we walk that he doesn't also walk. He doesn't get weary of the struggles we face, nor our tears and irrational fears. He keeps saying, "I will not forsake you." In this very moment, he is with you.

Dear Father,
Thank you for your faithful presence with me. I confess my fears and many worries to you. Teach me to live in this promise of your unfailing presence throughout the day so that I'm not rattled by what meets my eyes. I want to see you, as it were. Thank you that your truths always stand. Today, Father, I need to meet you afresh in this valley.
In Jesus's name, amen.

KEPT BY GOD

Day Two

Read Isaiah 43:2–4

When you pass through the waters, I will be with you; and through the rivers, they shall not overwhelm you; when you walk through fire you shall not be burned, and the flame shall not consume you. For I am the Lord your God… you are precious in my eyes, and honored, and I love you…

—Isaiah 43:2–4

A few years ago, we undertook a major renovation in our house that involved living elsewhere while the house was being rebuilt. We were moving out in a matter of days and had to sort through our belongings since we would be downsizing.

It was Saturday morning and we were having a garage sale. Our son had tried to take his life the previous week, but he was home now on a weekend pass. In addition, our dog had been poisoned and we weren't sure if he would live. It was stressful, to say the least.

There are times we feel like we are white-water rafting and no one is controlling the raft. We're simply being driven along by the raging current while trying to navigate dangerous rocks.

Against the backdrop of fear comes this tender promise of God to keep us safe when storms line up and just keep coming.

Notice how threatening the storms are. We're passing right through the deep waters; there is no footing. It's the same with the rushing rivers; they threaten to carry us away. Regarding the fire, we're right in the midst of it. We are not at arm's length from these storms! We're right in the thick of them.

Yet God is with us in each case. He is the one who keeps us from becoming overwhelmed by these scenarios, even when they all come at the same time. His presence alone keeps us. He is in the middle of the fire and the water with us.

Most precious of all is the tender word of God that explains why we are kept by him in such storms. The reason is that we are precious to him and are honoured in his sight. He loves you. That's why you don't go down in the storm.

Dear Father,
Thank you for your presence and enduring love for me and for the beautiful promises of Isaiah 43. I need to know that the waves will not sweep over me and the fire will not burn me. You will help me today, and for this I am so thankful. There is no road you will not walk with me today. Please give me every ounce of strength I will need for today.
In Jesus's name, amen.

HELPED BY GOD
Day Three
Read Psalm 121

I lift up my eyes to the hills. From where does my help come? My help comes from the Lord, who made heaven and earth.

—Psalm 121:1–2

Where do you look for help? We all need help. Solo fliers don't fare well through these kinds of storms. The gift of skilled and caring help is a resource we would never turn down, because we feel out of our depth so often.

So where do you look for help? As today's verse says, *"I lift up my eyes to the hills…"* Is it from the hills that help comes? It's just as likely that harm comes from the hills than help. The hills are a source for all kinds of unpredictable forces. No guarantees of help come from there.

What is significant here is the act of lifting our eyes. Our eyes can easily become downcast because we're discouraged over our loved one. Maybe they have become fixed on the ditch these ones find themselves in.

The longer we look, the more discouraging it becomes. Perhaps you're just staring straight ahead, through an act of sheer determination putting one foot in front of the other and keeping on. Your joy has vanished. Why not lift your eyes up above all your challenges, and look to God?

Our help comes from the Lord, not the hills but the maker of the hills. He made the heavens and the earth. He spoke and they came into being when everything was formless and void. He doesn't need an encouraging situation in order to create a good outcome. He can bring good out of sheer chaos. He can help.

Another piece of good news is that anyone can lift their eyes up and look to God. Even a child can do that. It is an acknowledgement of dependence. It is also where contentment is found, by looking upward to the one who loves you perfectly. That is also the place of rest because in lifting our eyes to God, we instinctively move over and let him to do the heavy lifting.

Dear Father,
You alone are my helper. Forgive me for looking so intently on this broken situation. I lift my eyes to you for I know that in you alone is help. You will help me. I rest in you. I trust you with this situation. Your intervention is the only thing that could truly bring about real change. Thank you for being both able and willing to help. Give me eyes to see what you are doing. I will be watching for you today.
In Jesus's name, amen.

STRENGTHENED BY GOD
Day Four
Read Isa 40:28–31

He gives power to the faint, and to him who has no might he increases strength.

—Isaiah 40:29

At our church, we would gather street-involved people for a meal on Saturday evenings and a worship service for anyone interested. The song "Amazing Grace" was like the Hallelujah chorus for them. They would sometimes stand and remove their hats while we sang. They bowed low before God, believing that God wasn't lucky to have them. They were utterly dependent on him. Many were addicts and had a long list of personal failures. No entitlement there.

Isaiah says that God gives power to the weak. To the one who has no might, he increases strength. It takes an enormous amount of strength to walk the sober road; that is a power that doesn't reside in the heart of the addict. Perhaps there are a few who have turned successfully away from addiction by sheer will. In our experience, such a victory is most often gained through an encounter with God and is sustained day by day through his strength. This passage breathes hope and life into anyone who has a loved one ensnared by addiction or mental illness.

The great thing about this promise is that the admission of weakness becomes the gateway for an experience in God's strength. Those who wait for the Lord in the place of weakness experience a renewal of their strength. Weakness doesn't disqualify anyone; it is the very key that unlocks the strength we long for.

Our weakness qualifies us for his strength. This applies equally to our loved one. We are all out of our depth. To come humbly before God with the admission of our great need of him opens the way. He is drawn to humility, yours and your loved one's.

How often do you feel weary and without strength? Depleted before the day has even begun, you wonder seriously how you will make it through to the end. As you wait upon God in the humble admission of your need, he will surely increase your strength—and he will do the same for your loved one if they have ears to hear it.

Dear Father,
Thank you for your promise of strength and power. This path is so tiring, and I cannot do it without you. I ask for your strength to fill me today. Walk with me and show me the way. I pray that my loved one would know the reality of this passage as well. I pray that my loved one would put their hope in you.
In Jesus's name, amen.

LED BY GOD
Day Five
Read Deuteronomy 31:8

It is the Lord who goes before you. He will be with you; he will not leave you or forsake you. Do not fear or be dismayed.

—Deuteronomy 31:8

I'm not sure there is a promise that encourages me more than this one. I have clung to this word while sitting beside a hospital bed or making yet another trip to pick up our son when he was in terrible shape.

To walk into these impossible situations, we must know deep in our hearts that God walks before us. Since this is unfamiliar territory, we don't know the way. We don't know how to get out of this deep and ongoing crisis. Our attempts to fix the situation or the other person are met with resistance and can make matters worse.

There is no formula to refer to and no GPS to pull up. Only God can guide us to our destination. He knows the way through, and he will instruct us. Though we cannot control our loved one or their response, God will guide us step by step. We believe in a speaking God and, though we don't hear him perfectly, he promises to guide us.

In addition, he protects us. This is hostile territory, entirely unwelcoming. There are countless dangers here and we don't even know what they are. Our only hope of navigating this pathway with all its unseen peril is if God goes before us.

This promise also means that he sticks around for the mess as it unfolds. He has the stomach for whatever we must face. He will not walk out on us.

The verse closes by saying, *"Do not fear or be dismayed"* (Deuteronomy 31:8). The fact that God goes before us has greater effect in our lives than anything that could cause us fear or dismay. No doubt you face situations where you have plenty of reasons to be afraid and deeply discouraged. Yet this promise remains, true and intact. God knows what you and I do not. We are wise to trust him.

Many times, we have to simply receive this in faith because there is zero reason to hope from what our human eyes can see. Yet we do not prefer the alternative and we cannot turn our back on what God promises us.

Dear Father,
Thank you for your guiding hand. Your presence steadies me. With so many dangers on this journey, I trust in you alone to guide me and protect my loved one. Calm my many fears today. May your peace flood my mind and heart. Thank you for walking before me and never abandoning me on this journey. I am lost without you.
In Jesus's name, amen.

PURSUING PEACE WHEN FEAR IS NEAR

Week Nine

Introduction

It's probably not possible for someone to walk with an addict, or someone struggling with mental illness, and not face fear. I remember my loved one telling me he woke up one day with huge bruises on his hips. He had been heavily drinking the night before and stumbled back to his residence. He had a vague memory of being hit by a taxi. The entire story was so foggy in his memory that he couldn't recount it. Stories like this illicit fear from any parent. When someone you love is out of control, they're at the mercy of whatever is around them.

The first time our son was admitted to the hospital and confessed that he didn't want to live, they put him in "lockdown." It reminded me of a prison. He was put into a large room together with many others also in crisis. There were no pictures on the walls. It was dimly lit. Nobody spoke to each other; each one was in their own world. The nursing station was behind heavy glass and locked doors in the middle of the room. From there, a few nurses watched over all these desperately troubled souls.

This was our introduction to "lockdown." It was terrifying.

We went home that day and reflected on the people we had seen there. They were struggling deeply with mental illness and some with addiction. Later, I sat on my front deck and thought about our son whom we had dedicated to God while he was still in my womb. I prayed, "God, is this really the future you have for our son?" In his mercy, God spoke to me: *"When I am in your son's future, everything is different."* I wept with relief.

The journey would last several more years, but I held on to God's promise to me on this day and it gave me peace.

One can purchase nearly anything in a store, but never resting peace. That comes from God alone.

WHEN GOD SEEMS UNCONCERNED
Day One
Read Mark 4:35–41

And he awoke and rebuked the wind and said to the sea, "Peace! Be still!" And the wind ceased, and there was a great calm.

—Mark 4:39

I have paddled through very high waves in a canoe, and I've seen my son at his worst. The height of the waves we paddled through doesn't begin to touch the fear that gripped my heart as we watched our son struggling under the burden of addiction.

Where can we go to find peace when our loved ones are destroying their lives? Watching is often unbearable.

The disciples knew boating, considering some were fishermen. Storms were not foreign. After a long day with crowds of people, Jesus was tired. When he got to the boat, he climbed to the back and fell fast asleep, seemingly unaware of the storm raging around them.

How could anyone sleep through that? Is it possible to experience peace during storms?

First, it is important to note that this story opens with Jesus saying, *"Let us go across to the other side"* (Mark 4:35). This meant that they would reach the other side. Though fierce storms may come and threaten to take you down, Jesus still intends to get you to your destination. The goal has not changed.

Second, storms don't have to rattle us. The storm didn't bother Jesus. He doesn't have the expectation that we won't go through storms. We often assume that with Jesus in the boat, storms will not be our portion. That is not the case. Storms aren't an indication that we lack spirituality or even that we did something wrong. Storms sometimes just arise out of nowhere.

Third, though Jesus did in the end still the storm, he was dismayed by the disciples' lack of faith. Given all they had seen Jesus do, he'd expected that their faith would grow, and their fear dissipate. When that didn't happen, he was troubled. The storm didn't trouble him; their lack of faith did.

He is with us in the boat. Can we trust him, even with the wind howling? Rather than being irritated by his seeming passivity, why not rest in his confidence to get you where he said he would?

Dear Father,
Thank you for your presence with me in this storm. Thank you for the certainty that you will get me to the destination you have promised. Forgive me for my impatience with your seeming passivity. Bring to me and my loved one the kind of peace that comes from you alone. In Jesus's name, amen.

POWERFUL PEACE
Day Two
Read John 14:26–27

But the Helper, the Holy Spirit, whom the Father will send in my name, he will teach you all things and bring to your remembrance all that I have said to you. Peace I leave with you; my peace I give to you. Not as the world gives do I give to you. Let not your hearts be troubled, neither let them be afraid.
—John 14:26–27

If you were going to climb Mount Everest, you would hire a sherpa to carry your gear, for the way forward is steep and challenging.

Jesus tells us here that the Holy Spirit is to us "the Helper." He is named that. He dwells in our lives, reminding us of truths we knew but may have forgotten due to the intensity of the conflict. He also teaches us many things that are crucial to finding our way through the complexity of the issues we deal with.

Everything seems new in these sorts of challenges, and we lack reference points. We often don't understand where God is in them and easily lapse into self-condemnation. The Holy Spirit brings us the reality of Jesus and teaches us many things essential to this journey. What strikes us is his kindness, patience, and tender love.

In earlier times, he dwelt intimately only with a few key people, usually leaders. That is no longer the case. He now lives in the hearts of all who love him. Social status, age, intelligence, and skill level aren't issues. God is right in our midst—this is no arm's length relationship—enabling us to do things we never otherwise could have; before, they were only hopeful aspirations.

When he speaks peace to you, this is not a mild suggestion you somehow have to work up. Peace comes to you. It comes particularly as you humbly read the Word of God, receiving what it says. Very quietly, the Holy Spirit brings us the peace of Jesus. Since peace finds its source in him, it comes even in the worst situations and continues though our challenging circumstances haven't changed even slightly. This peace runs underneath all our troubles like a steady river and sustains us.

Dear Father,
Thank you for sending Jesus to die for me. Forgive me for every way in which I have broken your law. Come and take up residence in my life. Fill me with Your Holy Spirit. Thank you for the promise of peace. I humbly receive it. Help me to follow you. Give me all that is needed for the challenges I will face today. Thank you that I never walk alone.
In Jesus's name, amen.

PEACE KNOWING GOD HEARS OUR PRAYERS
Day Three
Read Joshua 1:9

Have I not commanded you? Be strong and courageous. Do not be frightened, and do not be dismayed, for the Lord your God is with you wherever you go.

—Joshua 1:9

Joshua was given a massive task and faced intimidating odds. As we face the daily challenges in our own lives and the life of our loved one, we too are up against what often seems impossible.

Bill and I have worked with many addicts over the years on the streets of Toronto. Our church does many things to reach out to them. Not uncommonly, we discover these individuals to be sons and daughters of parents who love God. Sometimes, though not always, they speak of their upbringing fondly and even longingly. They wish they could get back there but the way seems shut to them. Truly, only God can do it.

We often have the sense that we are the answer to the broken-hearted prayers of parents somewhere with these individuals. This is confirmed for us in the periodic phone calls we field from parents all across our nation who believe their children are in Toronto, addicted and in trouble. They send us photos and ask us to watch out for them.

Often when we speak with these dear kids, they are unusually receptive to the grace of God. Even the sight of the cross can bring tears to their eyes. Though their lives are so shattered and the control of addiction so strong, they reach back to God with hope. They may falter along the way, but for our part we will never stop hoping and praying for the grace of God to deliver them.

Your prayers are not wasted; they make a *huge* difference, though you may not see it. Though the day may seem dark, thank God for his unfailing presence and pray diligently for your loved one. Do not be terrified or discouraged. God is with you, as he is with your loved one. It is in this knowledge that we find peace.

Dear Father,
Thank you for your presence. Keep me from the terror and discouragement regarding my loved one. As you are with me, I need not be afraid. Calm every fear and replace it with your peace. Lead me into the next thing you would have me say or do in this situation. As you are with me, would you manifest your gracious presence to my loved one? Deliver this one from all evil and set them on a new path. Thank you for all you are doing, seen and unseen.
In Jesus's name, amen.

PEACE KNOWING YOU MATTER TO GOD
Day Four
Read Isaiah 43:1

But now thus says the Lord, he who created you, O Jacob, he who formed you, O Israel: "Fear not, for I have redeemed you; I have called you by name, you are mine."

—Isaiah 43:1

It is a great compliment when someone you have only met once remembers your name. It makes a person feel important, even honoured.

God thought it important to remind his people, who were in a very low spot, that he knew them by name. He takes them back to their first steps as a people, long before they were a nation. He says that he is the one who formed them. He also redeemed them, a reference to a massive rescue operation during which he drew them out of hopeless slavery. Finally, he indicates that he called them.

By three different and great works, God showed the depth of his relationship with them. He would never let them go, though they felt alone.

When we feel alone, we may become desperate. We act irrationally or say things we might regret. There is no peace in that place of loneliness. It's hard not to feel forgotten.

What draws us out of that desperation is the reminder that we really do matter to God. He formed us. He knows our frailty and our limits. You can trust him in this, as he won't let you be drawn into difficulty beyond what you can manage. He knows when the climb is too steep and the way too long. He will give you a bench along the way to rest, even if only for a few minutes.

Remember, he redeemed us. This is proof that we are bound to him and he to us through Christ. Your present hardships, and even how you perform in them, will never nullify that strong relationship. He calls us by name and draws us into a future and a hope which can never be taken from us. His call is irrevocable.

You matter to God. Knowing that brings peace. Allow God to write that on your heart.

Dear Father,
Thank you for forming, redeeming, and calling me. I find security in your love and peace in knowing that I belong to you. The fact that I am personally on your radar sets my heart at ease. Help me in my weakness. Give me rest along the weary road and sustain me in the journey. Reveal yourself to my loved one. I am so thankful that you know their name also.
In Jesus's name, amen.

KEPT IN PEACE BY GOD
Day Five
Read Isaiah 26:3

You keep him in perfect peace whose mind is stayed on you, because he trusts in you.

—Isaiah 26:3

Perfect peace! It sounds inviting. Everyone longs for it. Many would say that it's only found on a quiet vacation when the pressures of life are lifted. This may be our experience, but what about all the times when that isn't an option?

This is a peace God keeps us in. Such a peace comes because he intervenes. It has nothing to do with how tranquil your environment is. You can find this peace just as likely when you're storm-tossed as when all is quiet. Why? Because it's a function of God working.

Though God's power keeps a person in perfect peace, stepping into that experience requires our minds to be set on him in an act of trust. The alternative is to obsess on our loved one's imperfections or our various fears over where this thing could go.

I remember one of my last trips to pick up my son. He was drunk, angry, and in great misery. How does one keep perfect peace in this situation? I asked Jesus to come along with me. He was always my companion on such trips. The thought of going without him was unimaginable. His presence brought me peace though everything around me was dark and grievous. I held onto everything I knew to be true about God and his promises—and I was kept by God's power and peace.

At our trailer, we have a dock and an inflatable pink flamingo. Sometimes I tie the flamingo to the dock and read. As long I'm tethered to the dock, I feel secure and have a peaceful reading experience. If that tether breaks, my reading quickly turns to anxiety.

In the same way, the mind that is tethered to God and trusts him is one that has great peace.

One of the simplest and most powerful ways to make this a reality for you is to take a scripture like this one and memorize it. Your mind will automatically be drawn down new paths. Peace will come to your heart.

Dear Father,
Thank you for your word and great selection of beautiful promises that are mine to gather up like a bouquet of flowers. Thank you for your willingness to walk into whatever today holds and for the peace that you promise will be mine. I need strength and wisdom for today, Jesus. Thank you for being a faithful Lord and Saviour.
In Jesus's name, amen.

THE CONTROL FACTOR
Week Ten
Introduction

Alcoholics Anonymous has a slogan that says, "Let go and let God." This slogan has a different meaning to the recovering addict than for those of us who are walking this journey alongside them. To the addict, it is an invitation to admit they cannot control their addiction, which therefore opens the way to truly accept the help of God. For us, though, our temptation is to rescue, fix, and control. We do it because this person is clearly not doing well. Our reasoning is obvious: "Someone has to step in, don't they? Surely we need to get involved and make some good decisions for them here."

Truly, there are times when we do need to step in. However, this journey has many moments when we must let go and trust God to do what we shouldn't or couldn't do. We cannot control our loved one; that is not given to us. Only God can tinker in their heart. The sooner we stop our many efforts of trying to fix them, the sooner we will begin to truly reach out to God to do what only he can do. Until then, it is questionable whether we are really trusting him.

There is another saying I came across in a support group I attended: "I didn't cause it and I can't cure it." In my mind, I added, "Let go and trust God." I put this over my sink where I could see it often.

I battle deeply with needing to fix the problem, any problem, forgetting that it's not mine to fix. I love to fix things. Fixing things just makes my world a happier place. However, many things are out of my reach, including this loved one who is so dear to my heart. It's counterintuitive to take my hands off, yet I must.

I'm not responsible for this person's recovery. Furthermore, my efforts to control him could make matters worse.

This week we will focus on letting go and trusting God. There is rest available to us as we receive what God has for us.

UNPACKING THE URGE TO RESCUE
Day One
Read Psalm 37

Delight yourself in the Lord, and he will give you the desires of your heart.

—Psalm 37:4

As much as your loved one needs to figure out why they do what they do, we need to figure out why we keep trying to fix them. For me, I believed if I just continued to do this—whatever "this" is—he would stop drinking. Maybe it's because it was too painful watch the destructive behaviour and it seemed impossible to sit idly by.

Probably the greatest motivation behind our controlling behaviour is fear; we fear where this thing could go, and we need to stop the crazy train. Maybe it's an issue of respectability; what's going on is an embarrassment to the family and our intervention is an effort to cover up the shame.

It could also be that my husband and I saw our role with our son differently from what it was when he was small; we were still rescuing him as we did then.

Whatever the reason, it's important to reflect and understand why we feel so compelled to step in and fix them.

Delighting yourself in the Lord will produce better results. This person will receive the desires of their heart. To what degree do your wearying efforts actually bring about the desires of your heart? God changes us as he does our loved ones. It is better to rest in him, laying our deep concerns before him in quiet prayer, than it is to try to help our loved one along by our many rescuing efforts.

To delight yourself in the Lord is to take time to rest in all of who he is. It's like stopping to gaze at a beautiful sunset, taking it all in such that it affects your mind and you spontaneously say, "Wow, God, you are amazing!" I have found that as I take time to delight my heart in him, a quiet shift takes place in me.

When you do the same, you will find it much easier to commit your way to the Lord and pull back from patterns that are unprofitable.

Dear Father,
You are worthy of all my praise and worship. I delight in your faithful love and great power. Forgive me for all my efforts at trying to fix my loved one. I see that only you can do that. It is definitely not given to me. I trust my loved one to you and ask that you help me to walk under your instruction and act in this relationship in ways that are truly profitable.
In Jesus's name, amen.

SO WHAT IS GOD'S PART AND WHAT IS MINE?

Day Two

Read John 14:1

Let not your hearts be troubled. Believe in God; believe also in me.

—John 14:1

Life is seldom neat and tidy, regardless of the season. Trouble comes to all. Our response is important. Jesus told us not to let our hearts be troubled. When the heart becomes troubled by our loved one, our response often isn't great. Next thing we know, we step in and try to fix them. Fear is near and we need to act!

Coming to grips with what is God's part and what is ours matters. It's easy to step into what is God's part since he sometimes seems to be a little too inactive. We want to help God, which is a complete role reversal.

God alone can touch a heart. That is not given to us. He alone saves—a work that he is constantly doing, even in our own lives. He understands our loved one. When they're ready to stop and ask God for help, God will be there. It is much better for us to rest in God. Our prayers for them are the best we can do. Prayer makes a difference, whether we see it or not.

What made the disciples' hearts troubled was that Jesus said he would be leaving them. Anticipating this change brought fear and anxiety. This didn't seem in any way at all a desirable change. They felt alone and even abandoned until Jesus explained why it was to their advantage that he left. He also explained that he would not leave them alone.

We too react in unhealthy ways in our relationship with our loved one because we feel it's all on us.

When life makes little sense and we cannot see our way through, the words of Christ still call out to us: *"Let not your hearts be troubled. Believe in God…"* Stay away from what is his alone and stick with what is yours: to trust him.

Dear Father,
Thank you for your presence with me. Forgive me for the many things I do out of anxiety and fear, thinking I am alone. Forgive me for acting like I am God and doing things that aren't given me to do and failing to do the main things I should be doing. I choose to trust you. I know you're doing more in my loved one than meets the eye. Bring peace to my troubled heart.
In Jesus's name, amen.

MISGUIDED COMPASSION

Day Three

Read Jeremiah 17:7–8

Blessed is the man who trusts in the Lord, whose trust is the Lord. He is like a tree planted by water, that sends out its roots by the stream, and does not fear when heat comes, for its leaves remain green, and is not anxious in the year of drought, for it does not cease to bear fruit.

—Jeremiah 17:7–8

I confess that I struggle in gardening. Thriving plants are not my specialty. I am learning, though.

Our lives are pictured here as a thriving plant, even in adversity. There are things we do, however, that undermine our own spiritual vitality.

Allowing unbridled compassion to consistently rule the day is one of them. Compassion must be tempered by wisdom and the fear of God. Compassion alone can lead a person to do things that aren't helpful, though they may be compassionate.

Repeatedly rescuing a loved one caught in addiction, thinking that your compassion will turn the tide, is generally a vain hope. They need to feel the consequences of their choices. Unless they do, healing will evade them. What follows will be ongoing confusion in your home and it will deplete you.

By contrast, the one who trusts in the Lord has a fruitful life and does not wither. To trust in the Lord is to pray and take instructions from him. He is our leader and trusted guide. Sometimes it's best to step in, but not always. If your only pattern is to rescue your loved one, it's unlikely that God is leading you. We need God to help us help our loved ones, even when it means stepping back. We choose to allow our roots to sink more deeply into God as we wait and trust. He becomes our source.

There were times when we went out to find our boy and bring him home, but not always. We never knowingly financed his addiction. We raised topics we thought to be wise, but at other times we felt prevented by God from raising certain topics. Sometimes emotion got the best of us, but we tried seriously to take our lead from God.

Difficult as it is, compassion must take its cues from God. That is where fruitfulness lies.

Dear Father,
Teach me your ways. Forgive me for being compulsive in my compassion. Give me quietness of spirit to be still and listen to you. Then give me the courage to obey. I need your wisdom and peace. I choose to walk under your instruction and wait. Fill me with courage.
In Jesus's name, amen.

LOVE VERSUS THE CONTROL FACTOR
Day Four
Read Psalm 143:7–8

Let me hear in the morning of your steadfast love, for in you I trust. Make me know the way I should go, for to you I lift up my soul.

—Psalm 143:8

As I read this psalm, my mind is flooded by memories of the morning after one of our son's drinking binges. Despair and exhaustion greeted me. The psalmist, however, cries out differently: *"Let me hear in the morning of your steadfast love…"*

When the day feels gloomy and your heart is heavy, it would be wise to request of God, "Father, show me your love!" The Father's love reaches to the highest heaven and the lowest hell. It's not diminished for you or your loved one! Our experience of his love may not feel like that.

When we drift from a growing experience in the love of God, we become rescuers of our loved one and probably quite controlling. Fear is close at hand. It is the love of God that quiets us and can deliver us from behaving unwisely. However, love drives out fear; it replaces it. How can penetrating fear stand in the face of perfect love? It cannot. As one grows, the other diminishes. It can be no other way.

God's love is not meant to be arm's length from us or an experience we had in the distant past. Rather, morning by morning, we fold ourselves into the love of God and rest in his tender care, both for us and our loved one.

Then we are ready to listen for instructions regarding taking the next steps with our loved one, says the psalmist. Listening to God for what is profitable in this relationship grows out of an experience in his love. We are not jittery because of anxiety as we wait in prayer but rather quiet, for we know his eye is upon us and we are precious to him. We will not hear him while our minds race out of fear.

That is not the case, though, when we have stilled and quieted ourselves in his love. Then we will hear him, and hear him we must. Only he knows the way forward with our loved one. We take our cues from him.

Dear Father,
Thank you for your love, which is steady and unchanging. Reveal your love to me today. Without that, I feel thin and withered. Steady my soul in your love and let my fear dissipate. I want to hear your voice calling me and directing me. Only you know the way forward here. Show me the way through this wilderness. I wait for your instructions.
In Jesus's name, amen.

PLAYING GOD
Day Five
Read Matthew 6:34

Therefore do not be anxious about tomorrow, for tomorrow will be anxious for itself. Sufficient for the day is its own trouble.

—Matthew 6:34

To worry is not hard. No one needs to attend a seminar to find out how to worry! Honestly, worry comes effortlessly to me.

During our journey with our son, I often found myself thinking, "Where is his life going?" or "I wonder if he will drink tonight?" Or maybe, "Will he overdose on his medication to get it over with and just finish the battle?" I can recall so many of my worries, as they all visited my mind so many times.

Anxiety is never the end of the road. What flows out of anxiety is behaviour that forces the situation to some desired end. It is not behaviour borne out of waiting on God, but out of fear. We cannot bear the thought of where our loved one is heading, so we can become heavy-handed.

Forcefulness, even if we mean well, seldom wins the day. It tends to turn our loved one against us. There's no wisdom in it. Your loved one can sense this. An addict reads people; it's survival for them. We are playing God and we don't do it well. We need to travel upstream and deal with the anxiety if we are to bring any wisdom to the table and act in helpful ways.

Jesus simply said, *"Therefore do not be anxious about tomorrow, for tomorrow will be anxious for itself."* Let's just focus on today. It's generally not given to us to know what tomorrow holds.

God has that in hand, though. It's far better to wait on him for instructions and comfort. Only he knows the way through this wasteland.

Wait on him through the morning. Then do it again as you move through the afternoon. Once more in the evening, and then at night. At times the thought of managing the whole day will be just too much. Take it hour by hour. God will give you his peace.

Dear Father,
Thank you for not leaving me. Forgive me for trying to do what is yours alone. Forgive me for my obsessive worrying. It changes my relationship with my loved one. I choose today to wait quietly on you. Instruct me in the way I should go. Deliver me from anxiety. Bring a different pattern into my life, one that waits quietly for you. Thank you that I am not without hope.
In Jesus's name, amen.

HOLDING ONTO FAITH
Week Eleven
Introduction

I was listening to a sermon last night. The preacher spoke about bringing tiny seeds of faith to the Lord. I found great comfort in these words. Holding onto faith in God, asking him to bless the food that is sitting in front of us, is easy. It's a little more challenging to believe when you have an empty table and bare cupboards.

As I reflect on the journey with our loved one, that is how it felt—the table was empty and the cupboards bare. I couldn't detect any sign of progress to inspire hope.

Have you ever felt that? Maybe that's how you feel now. Exhaustion and discouragement can make faith seem hard to come by. We know that God is merciful, and that he saves. So we continue to look to him. There is none other.

This week, let's focus on how to hold onto and grow in our faith even when there is little reason for hope from our vantage point. The Scriptures bring us hope and faith when our own storehouse is very low.

FAITH THAT BRINGS A LOVED ONE TO JESUS

Day One
Read Mark 2:1–12

And when Jesus saw their faith, he said to the paralytic, "Son, your sins are forgiven."

—Mark 2:5

This passage tells the delightful story of four men who brought a paralytic to Jesus against great odds. The crowd inside was huge, so creative options were needed; they hoisted their friend up onto the roof, then dug through and lowered him in front of Jesus. As expected, they gained an audience with Jesus, who then healed their friend.

Several things are to be noted here. First, your loved one may well not find their way to Jesus alone. They aren't so different from the paralytic. If you're waiting for them to get their act together and get themselves to Jesus, you'll probably be disappointed. Someone will need to carry them there—in prayer.

Second, you'll face great obstacles in this mission. People will discourage you. You may want to give up. However, you know enough about Jesus to press on. If your loved one isn't making obvious moves towards Jesus, you carry them there in prayer. Present them before God in the name of Jesus and don't let anything stop you.

Third, Jesus sees your faith. In the story, Jesus notices the friends' faith, not the man's. Their faith is seen in how insistent they are to get their friend to Jesus despite every obstacle. Jesus notices this about you. He sees your determination in prayer, which will not take no for an answer. This kind of insistence knows that only Jesus can help.

Finally, Jesus heals the paralytic, but he does it in a rather roundabout way. He sees the real problem and forgives the man of his sins. The physical healing is only a byproduct of this much greater healing of the soul. Jesus knows these things.

As you bring your loved one to him in prayer, rest assured that he will deal with the main thing. The addiction is only a symptom of that which is deeper. God hears your prayers. Stay with it.

Dear Father,
I present my loved one before you in the name of Jesus. Forgive me for losing heart in the face of innumerable obstacles. I know that only you can help this one who is precious to me. Help me to persevere and not lose hope. I place my confidence in your word and simply wait for you. Thank you for hearing my prayer.
In Jesus's name, amen.

WHO EXACTLY ARE YOU TRUSTING?

Day Two

Read 2 Corinthians 5:7, 2 Timothy 1:12

…for we walk by faith, not by sight…

—2 Corinthians 5:7

But I am not ashamed, for I know whom I have believed, and I am convinced that he is able to guard until that day what has been entrusted to me.

—2 Timothy 1:12

Our hope must be in God, not people. People can disappoint, but God never does. He is true to his word every time. Walking by faith and not by sight only makes sense when the one you're trusting is worthy and able to accomplish what you're believing him for. God alone is up for this task.

Confidence is so important. To have full confidence in God is to be a person at rest, even though there would be many disappointments all around you. Once you set your eyes on God, the rest doesn't matter so much. You're simply waiting for him to save.

The act of committing things to God is a function of that confidence. Many of us have dedicated our children to God when they were young. We do that because we trust in him. However, as the years go on, life becomes complicated and our loved ones sometimes find themselves in bondage and hopelessness. Those acts of commitment when they were young seem too far away now, only relevant in less troubling times perhaps.

Is that really the case, though? Were those acts of commitment not done in faith, believing that God would accomplish them? To be sure, our parenting is never perfect, and our kids make their own choices. Yet God is faithful. Why don't we come back to those earlier dedications and pray like we did then, in simple faith that God, who is above all, is able to guard what has been entrusted to us, namely our loved one? We have no reason to let go of that act of dedication. God has not changed.

The temptation to give up on prayer is strong when we walk alongside someone struggling with mental illness or addiction. From where we stand, it can seem utterly hopeless. Yet when we fix our eyes on God, and lift them off the people around us, we will find rest for our souls.

Dear Father,
I trust in you. Only you can save. Forgive me for shifting my confidence onto people. All power is yours, as is lovingkindness. Would you save my loved one? Hear again the acts of dedication I made in earlier times. Hear and act, O God. Calm the fears that grip my heart. I ask for your peace.
In Jesus's name, amen.

HOLDING STEADY AMID BAD NEWS
Day Three
Read Psalm 112:6–8

For the righteous will never be moved... He is not afraid of bad news; his heart is firm, trusting in the Lord. His heart is steady; he will not be afraid...

—Psalm 112:6–8

One evening when we had guests over for dinner, our son hadn't come home when he had said he would. We knew immediately that he was out drinking. Both of our hearts were on edge while we quietly called out to God to calm our fears once more. That familiar knot was back while I tried to listen to our guests. Somewhere out in this large city, our loved one had fallen back into a self-destructive pattern—and there was nothing we could do to stop it.

Nobody likes bad news. There's no easy way to receive it. Even if you try to play certain mind games to brace yourself or lessen the impact, those strategies amount to very little. The situation packs a punch that tends to wear you down. Bad news is always bad news, no matter how often it comes.

Bad news, however, is never the end of the story for the righteous, and in the end we learn not to fear it. In fact, even if you've lost your footing momentarily because of it, God steadies you.

A certain unexplainable comfort and resilience comes to the righteous, for those whose trust is in God. The peace of God amid bad news touches the deepest part of our souls and eases pain, taking the strength out of fear. Bad news loses its strength because of the presence of God and our faith in him.

We can also rest knowing that God makes a difference in the situation. We call out to him because we believe he can do what we cannot. We believe that God will carry us, and he watches over our loved one and can bring good out of bad news.

God is always greater than the bad news. The power and goodness of God runs much deeper. It is always wise to immediately put our trust in God when bad news comes.

Dear Father,
You hold the earth in your hands. I rest my loved one's life at your throne. Whatever lies ahead, I know that you will meet me and that my loved one is always in your view. Thank you for your comfort. Thank you for steadying my heart and taking the strength out of my fear. Keep my loved one safe; protect them when they cannot protect themselves. Deliver them from evil. Fill me with your peace.
In Jesus's name, amen.

IT'S A MATTER OF ASKING
Day Four
Read 1 John 5:14–15

And this is the confidence that we have toward him, that if we ask anything according to his will he hears us. And if we know that he hears us in whatever we ask, we know that we have the requests that we have asked of him.

—1 John 5:14–15

Have you ever had to purchase something quite unique in nature and had a tough time finding it? You go to store and after store, yet you come up with nothing.

I once needed something very particular for our trailer. After trying four different stores, I went to a very specific one that sold everything having to do with trailers. I didn't even understand exactly what I was asking for, but the salesman did. He went into the storeroom and brought out exactly what I was looking for. I left feeling relieved and thankful.

We are told in Scripture that we can approach God's throne room with confidence and ask him anything according to his will. Knowing what to ask God is important. You have specific requests in your prayers as you look to intercede. It is important to be quite precise in your prayers to God, moving beyond vague generalities. Base your prayers on the promises and teachings of the word of God. It is not presumptuous to speak like that to God.

Admittedly, there are times when we don't know what to ask. Scripture teaches us that the Spirit of God helps us in those times and takes our prayers to a much deeper level before our Father in heaven, articulating in heaven exactly what is the will of God in the situation.

Yet it is wise for us to ask God how we should pray for our loved one. He will direct you and give specific thoughts and next steps which he wants to accomplish. This practice changes how we see prayer. In this way, prayer involves listening just as much as it does speaking. It is relational and full of hope. It is also very effective. We love effective!

Dear Father,
Thank you for hearing me when I come and sit before you day after day. Teach me your way. Show me from your word how I ought to pray for my loved one. Speak to me as I wait before you and show me what is the next thing you wish to do in the life of my life and the life of my loved one. Thank you for hearing my prayers and answering me.
In Jesus's name, amen.

WAIT FOR THE LORD
Day Five
Read Psalm 27:13–14

I believe that I shall look upon the goodness of the Lord in the land of the living! Wait for the Lord; be strong, and let your heart take courage; wait for the Lord!

—Psalm 27:13–14

What makes these verses so precious is that they are an expression of hope in God. We will see his goodness now, while we are alive. We know that our hope ultimately is heaven, to be with Jesus forever. In that place his comfort will be absolute and his peace unshakable, never to be removed. He himself will be there, wiping each tear from our eyes, manifesting his goodness to us day after day.

Yet that is not what this passage refers to. The Scriptures teach here that we will experience his goodness now, in the land of the living, in the very place where, at present, darkness often seems to reign.

The backdrop to these verses is the threat of death, both in the psalm and in our lives. The world of addiction and mental illness can sometimes be lived near death. Each time our loved one swam in those perilous waters, it seemed that death visited our home. It is dark and can be overwhelming, to say the least.

We purposely had to claim again the life of Jesus. Really, it's just the shadow of death, not death itself. Yet it feels like the real thing is so near, always threatening. In our weaker moments, we feared death would claim him. At those times, we remembered this passage and found hope again.

The psalmist is looking for the goodness of the Lord, which we also look for. We must train our eyes to search for it daily. From morning to evening, we must look for this one thing exactly in the place where there has been disappointment and darkness. We know it will show up because it is based on the good character of God, who will manifest himself in our experience as he promised. Hope then trickles in as we wait for God to reveal himself.

Dear Father,
As I look today into your beautiful face, I see your radiance and majesty. I call to mind that you are all-powerful and wise. I praise and worship you, for you are worthy of it. Thank you for bringing me today out of darkness into the land of the living where you dwell. Today I will wait for you to manifest your goodness to my loved one. Thank you for your love which never ceases.
In Jesus's name, amen.

WITHIN GOD'S REACH
Week Twelve
Introduction

It's easy to fall into the trap of doubting if this one whom we love so much will ever be rescued from the addiction which is swallowing up his life. For some of us, it's learning to navigate the seemingly endless challenges of one who lives daily with mental illness.

This doubt begins as a quiet, little thought. Given the often-repeated dark scenes that entered our home, the thought easily grew and took root. I had to remind myself that the Good Shepherd is always out, seeking the lost so that he might save them. He knows exactly where to find them—including your loved one.

Has God not renewed your hope over the years? What were those situations that seemed to be without solution? Somehow, as you prayed and trusted him, he reached down and moved a few pieces of the puzzle. You probably stood back and watched in amazement.

God has not changed. He is always at work, even in the life of your loved one right now.

Jesus, the Good Shepherd, is not like us. He is not given to becoming tired or discouraged. He doesn't weary of going out to search for the lost. He's not put off by how deep the pit is which they've fallen into, or how steep the climb will be to save them. He, unlike us, does not see the challenges in the rescue. He only sees the one who is lost. With him, nothing is impossible. This brings much comfort to my heart.

This week we will rest in this truth: our loved one is within God's reach.

DON'T DISQUALIFY YOURSELF

Day One
Read Daniel 6

I make a decree, that in all my royal dominion people are to tremble and fear before the God of Daniel, for he is the living God, enduring forever; his kingdom shall never be destroyed, and his dominion shall be to the end. He delivers and rescues; he works signs and wonders in heaven and on earth, he who has saved Daniel from the power of the lions.

—Daniel 6:26–27

Who doesn't love the story of Daniel and the lions' den? It's one of my favourites. Daniel was set up to fall by envious colleagues. The king was drawn into a trap from which he couldn't escape. The result was that Daniel was thrown into the lions' den, from which nobody could get out alive. However, God rescued him, shutting the mouths of the lions.

Seeing this dramatic deliverance, the king made a decree to his entire kingdom commanding all to fear God. The king had a revelation based on what he saw God do for Daniel. He came to all these conclusions about the character and work of God based purely on one act of rescue.

It's something of a mystery why we can look at great things God has done for someone else and think that he only does that for them. God's great deeds are often quite public, especially his acts of rescue. They're always done for the sake of the individual, though not only for their sake. God wants to strengthen the faith of others who will hear about the deed such that they too put their faith in him. We should take our cues from the king who sees this deed as an instruction for all to trust God implicitly.

We don't live in the day of lions' dens, but we are familiar with the destructive power of addiction and mental illness. We see where things could be headed with our loved one. We've heard the horror stories and read the statistics.

Who escapes from that lions' den? Why might we expect deliverance? Has God changed in his character? Has he weakened over time? Did he resign from being God Almighty? There is none beyond his reach. Perhaps he will do for you what he did for Daniel.

Dear Father,
Thank you for never changing, and for still seeking and saving the lost. Forgive me for excluding myself from the promises you have given me, disqualifying myself from the miracles you may want to do today. As you delivered Daniel, would you deliver my loved one from destruction? My loved one is not beyond your reach.
In Jesus's name, amen.

TRUSTING GOD WHEN THINGS LOOK IMPOSSIBLE
Day Two
Read Romans 4:17

...as it is written, "I have made you the father of many nations"—in the presence of the God in whom he believed, who gives life to the dead and calls into existence the things that do not exist.

—Romans 4:17

Abraham was old when God said to him, *"I have made you the father of many nations."* The only problem was that he and Sarah had no child. Yet Abraham believed God. Though things looked impossible, he trusted God and received what had been promised. They had a son when he was one hundred and she was ninety.

To believe God on a sunny day when everything is going our way is one thing. To trust him when your loved one is in active substance addiction is another matter. Though things look bleak, yet we lift our eyes to God. We look past the stumbling of our loved one up to God. God gives life to the dead and calls into existence the things that do not exist.

It doesn't matter to God whether a situation looks encouraging or not. He isn't affected by statistics or depressing stories. He doesn't care what the odds are. With him, nothing is impossible. When he has in mind something for your loved one, he simply calls it into existence. God is like that.

Faith is not hollow optimism. It is not believing what we want. It is believing what God wants. When he whispers a promise in your heart, hold onto it. Thank him for what he will do. Go to the Scriptures and live in them. If it's God whispering to you, it will never contradict Scripture and you will find many more promises there.

Faith can be a struggle. I never saw the day of sobriety come to either my dad or my brother. Both ended their lives actively addicted. Fear and panic can rise quickly when such a strong pattern is developing. Yet God gave us a promise for our son, and we believed it. Against all odds, God raised him up.

Dear Father,
Thank you that none are beyond your reach. Forgive me for thinking that my loved one is impossible and this situation beyond hope. Forgive me for obsessing on the wild choices of my loved one. Speak to my heart a promise for my loved one that I can cling to. Teach me from your word and I will hold onto that and wait for you to accomplish it.
In Jesus's name, amen.

IDENTIFYING WHAT KEEPS US FROM EXPERIENCING GOD'S DELIVERANCE

Day Three

Read Isaiah 59:1–2

> *Behold, the Lord's hand is not shortened, that it cannot save, or his ear dull, that it cannot hear; but your iniquities have made a separation between you and your God, and your sins have hidden his face from you so that he does not hear.*
>
> —Isaiah 59:1–2

Why does my loved one not get better? We long for health, even the slightest improvement. No doubt the issues involved in accurately discerning this situation are complex.

Two issues, however, are clear.

First, any delay in our loved one's improvement doesn't have to do with God's ability, as if he has somehow met his match here. It's not that he doesn't hear our prayers. Neither is it that he lacks what is needed to deliver our loved ones and set them free from what holds them captive. We may feel intimidated by the darkness of the situation, but God isn't subject to that. As he looks upon your loved one, he isn't trembling over what they'll do next. He doesn't see the insurmountable height of this great mountain; he sees you, as he does your loved one. Nothing has changed in his ability to save.

The second issue is also important to consider. There is a possibility that things we've done have broken God's laws, which prevents him from acting. This is only the case if we keep these sins hidden, as if we never committed them. As soon as we confess and ask forgiveness, that changes. He is, however, kept at bay by our unwillingness to come clean before him.

It is indeed very difficult to walk this unwanted journey and not make serious mistakes in what we say or how we respond. It's probably naïve for us to conclude that we have nothing to confess to God. Make it a regular practice, for the sake of your loved one, to confess your sin. You can have confidence then that there is nothing on your part standing in the way of God moving in the life of your loved one.

Dear Father,
Forgive me for the things I have said, done, and thought that have broken your law. Make me know your ways. Keep a lid over my mouth so I don't say things in frustration that will grieve you and bring greater difficulty to an already strained relationship. Fill me with wisdom. Thank you for your mercy. Thank you that nothing is too hard for you. Strengthen me for whatever is before me.
In Jesus's name, amen.

GOD IS THAT GREAT
Day Four
Read Psalm 139

Search me, O God, and know my heart! Try me and know my thoughts! And see if there be any grievous way in me, and lead me in the way everlasting!

—Psalm 139:23–24

Several aspects of this psalm strengthen our hope that our loved one is never beyond God's reach. The first is that God knows our loved ones completely (Psalm 139:1–3). Our loved ones are often a mystery to us, but never to God. We don't know what they're thinking about, where they go, or even where they are at this very moment. But God does.

Second, God places limits around our loved ones (Psalm 139:4–6). He hems them in. To be hemmed in is to be surrounded and restricted in how far one can move. Even when they push hard to live without restraint and in paths of their own making, they are still hemmed in. God keeps them from fully going down destructive paths, particularly as we pray.

Third, our loved ones can never escape God (Psalm 139:7–12). They may even be intent on that mission. There is, however, nowhere they could go where they can escape him. He is found not just in the heavens, but also in the depths of darkness. There is much we don't know of these places of darkness where our loved ones frequent in their brokenness. It matters not. God still holds authority in these places and isn't afraid of them. Our loved ones are never alone, even if they believe otherwise.

Fourth, we are reminded that God has a plan laid out for our loved ones when they're ready to take that path (Psalm 139:13–18). He knit them together skillfully while yet in their mother's womb and set the number of their days before one of them came to be. Though they are full of their own thoughts and plans, God's are not so easily set aside. In his love, he continues to call to them so they might walk in his ways. He is tenacious in his love.

Fifth, God deals with evil influences that are set against your loved one (Psalm 139:19–22). He takes a stand against people who would draw them away and harm them. This is a great comfort to us as we pray for our loved ones.

Dear Father,
Thank you for your great love and insight into all things. You know my loved one perfectly. I praise you because my loved one is not beyond your reach. Intervene, O Lord. I commit this one to your care.
In Jesus's name, amen.

CRYING OUT TO GOD
Day Five
Read Psalm 130

Out of the depths I cry to you, O Lord! O Lord, hear my voice! Let your ears be attentive to the voice of my pleas for mercy!

—Psalm 130:1–2

What is a cry? When children are small, there are different kinds of cries. Parents quickly learn to discern which is urgent. When a grownup truly cries out, there is always urgency. A cry grows out of desperation or deep sorrow. It comes out of "the depths," that place of darkness and confinement. It is a place where the threat is real and there is much to lose.

Learning to cry out to God in our anguish is critical. People will cry out, though not necessarily to God. When we pour out our hearts to a friend perhaps, it feels nice to be understood. It's unhealthy to keep things bottled up inside. We must express ourselves.

Without taking away from that, crying out to God in prayer brings us directly before the only one who can truly save. We cannot bear the thought of what is playing out before our eyes with our loved one. So we take hold of God and don't let him go. Though it may seem a little presumptuous to pray like that, it isn't. Your understanding is limited; God's understanding of the situation is complete and his power to act is without limit.

We don't cry out because he is hard of hearing or because we need to get his attention. We have his attention; that is never the problem. A cry to God is an expression of desperation and trust. Both of those are essential to prayer. These are not casual, armchair-type prayers. There is urgency here and much confidence that God will act.

As we cry out to God in prayer for our loved ones, we will also find peace and comfort. It's difficult to explain how that comes about out of a cry for mercy, but it does. God notices the urgency, the desperation, and he cares. He comforts us in our sorrow and manifests himself to us.

Dear Father,
Thank you for hearing my cry for mercy. I feel such desperation in my heart for my loved one. My loved one feels so much pain. Have mercy and heal this one. Restore my loved one. Protect him from evil and intervene. Give me your peace lest sorrow overwhelm me. Let me know your comfort. Thank you for your presence. I entrust my loved one to your care.
In Jesus's name, amen.

HOPEFUL LIVING ALONGSIDE THE MENTALLY ILL
Week Thirteen
Introduction

If you and I could get inside the mind of someone with mental illness, their perspective would be quite different from ours. It seems that they're looking out a window that is cracked, or even frosted in places. They can still see through the window, but not clearly. Imagine trying to describe what you're seeing through that window!

What if your hearing was also distorted because of crippling anxiety or depression? Again, they hear and perceive things differently than we do. A conversation which is entirely positive may suddenly take an unexpected turn. All at once, it may morph into something that is sharply negative or accusatory, even hopeless. You may be left wondering how this happened.

In our experience, where addictions are present, mental illness is seldom far away. When the two combine, it makes the person's mental state even worse. I witnessed this first with my brother and now my son. The alcohol doesn't mix well with mental health medications.

Living with mental illness is unquestionably challenging. So is living with someone who has such an illness. I remember how challenging it was trying to make family gatherings a good time for everyone. It was very stressful. I generally felt like we were all walking on eggshells, trying so hard not to set off any triggers for our loved one. When my brother, who struggled deeply with depression, would come for supper, he usually changed the oil in his car on our street. It was very odd. If you wanted to visit with him, it would have to be under the hood of his car.

We don't claim to be experts on mental illness. Neither would we contradict the advice of mental health practitioners. We do, however, want to bring encouragement and hope to those whose loved one struggles with it. Hope is in such short supply on this unwanted journey. Therefore, let us turn our attention to God, our only source for hope. He will encourage us.

WHY MAKING GOD YOUR REFUGE IS VITAL
Day One
Read Psalm 91:1–2

He who dwells in the shelter of the Most High will abide in the shadow of the Almighty. I will say to the Lord, "My refuge and my fortress, my God, in whom I trust."

—Psalm 91:1–2

Where do you find refuge when the way is difficult? Living alongside one who struggles with mental illness will put that to the test. If we don't make it a practice to make ourselves at home in all of who God is, we will be depleted very quickly by the realities of mental illness.

I don't think I noticed a particular Bible verse until I learned it had become my son's favourite: *"You have taken away my companions and loved ones. Darkness is my closest friend"* (Psalm 88:18, NLT).

Where will you find strength when the depression is so intense and the clouds so persuasive? How will you navigate diagnoses that are terrifying for both your loved one and yourself? What will be your resource when what you see going on inside this person is intense, dark, and altogether hopeless? How do you even find a smile when it's been months since you've seen one on the face of your loved one?

I recently went into a coffee shop and the owner gave me a business card that said "I am an oasis." I asked her who the "I am" is. I was wondering if she meant Jesus, the great I AM.

However, she said, "You are."

The entire coffee shop stopped talking at that moment and listened to our conversation.

I gave her card back and said, "I am not an oasis. I am a terrible oasis. My hiding place is in God Almighty. I go to him for rest, hope, and peace. I desperately need someone bigger, wiser, and abler than me to be my oasis!"

The woman seemed shaken by my response, but that was okay by me.

When dark shadows grow, we need an experience with God that is greater than the shadows. It's not unrealistic to expect that God will shine the light of his presence in your soul as you make him your refuge such that your spirit is buoyed up. Ask God to help you make him your refuge.

Dear Father,
In you I find my rest. I quiet my soul in your presence and linger there. Your love renews me.
My trust is in you. Thank you for your tender mercies and comforting presence. O God, shine your light into the soul of my loved one. Return life to this one who is precious to me.
In Jesus's name, amen.

A MEASURED RESPONSE
Day Two
Read Hebrews 13:6

So we can confidently say, "The Lord is my helper; I will not fear; what can man do to me?"
—Hebrews 13:6

Recently I was on Queen Street in Toronto when I noticed two young girls in conflict. One was yelling and acting aggressively towards her friend. She was tugging at the girl as they walked, unaware that people were watching. Nor did she clue in that her friend was frightened and wanted to get away from her.

It's not uncommon for those with mental illness to be unaware of how their behaviour affects those around them. Though I have always enjoyed having my loved one around, he could make me feel anxious and overwhelmed because of the confusion he often brought with him.

He was unaware of how his skyrocketing anxiety affected me. I could be made to feel on edge quickly, like when he didn't eat. He had no idea that his pessimism would come like a cloud and fill the home. When he failed to take his meds, anxiety filled me. To gently remind him was to invite him to angrily ask me to leave him alone. I had to stop trying to manage his meds.

How we respond in these situations is important. Our loved ones' actions are often not measured; they are extreme. Our reactions, though, must be measured. We need responses that come from God. We are wise to make him our help and wait upon him.

The words that come to my mind at this moment are *breathe* and *receive*. To breathe is to slow down, not panic, not feel that we must fix our loved one or even rescue them. We cannot hear God when we ourselves are overwhelmed with anxiety and fear. We don't have to respond to everything. Simply listen and nod. Breathe. Rest in God and know that he holds you in his loving care.

To receive from God is to acknowledge that we don't have what is needed in this situation and must get help from him. We also have deep confidence that he will give it to us. In moments of quiet trust, your Father in heaven hears your prayer and will give you what is needed to respond with wisdom.

Dear Father,
Thank you for your help today. Forgive me for failing to wait upon you for responses to my loved one. Lead me in heaven's wisdom and give me your strength to be measured in my response. Deliver me from everything extreme and dramatic. Give me a steady voice and unfailing love. May your peace rest upon me and my loved one.
In Jesus's name, amen.

FINDING A SAFE PLACE
Day Three
Read Romans 8:35–39

…in all these things we are more than conquerors through him who loved us. For I am sure that [nothing]… will be able to separate us from the love of God in Christ Jesus our Lord.

—Romans 8:37–39

Have you ever been invited to a party where you feel a bit out of place? You feel honoured to be invited but don't know many people there. You look for someone who might be willing to talk to you or include you, but it's not happening. As a result, you feel uncomfortable, perhaps even vulnerable. Where do you stand? What should you do?

This scene reminds me of what it often feels like to live with someone who struggles with mental illness. You need to find that safe, quiet place to stand amid the unpredictability and uncertainty of what confronts you day by day.

Mental illness, particularly when it's combined with addiction, can bring considerable confusion into your life, such that it is difficult to find a safe place, even though it's your own home. Substances that feed the addiction don't mix well with mental health medications and thus tend to make the individual's situation worse. Paranoia and delusions may seem to rule the day. Perspectives are skewed; what is real to your loved one seems strange to you. The most difficult part of it all is that you often become the target. You look for a safe place to stand, some solid rock that gives you firm footing to maintain clear thinking.

The safe place is this: nothing will ever separate you from the measureless love of God that is in Christ Jesus. Though this path you're on has so many twists, turns, and setbacks, this truth remains as your unchanging assurance. God's love for you holds steady. Nobody can take it from you. To rest in that knowledge is to find safety and quiet in the very core of your being.

Furthermore, overwhelming victory is ours through Christ. Delusions don't win the day in the end. With Christ's help, we find our way through the changing winds of adversity. God strengthens us and knows the way through. Will he not guide us? In this we can rest.

Dear Father,
I thank you for your unchanging love. Everywhere else I look, I see shifting sand. But in you I find unfailing love. Fill me with the knowledge of your love and give me a deeper experience in it. Help me to not be thrown off by what is going on around me. Give me understanding and wisdom.
In Jesus's name, amen.

THERE IS PURPOSE TO YOUR PAIN
Day Four
Read 2 Corinthians 1:3–7

Blessed be the God and Father of our Lord Jesus Christ, the Father of mercies and God of all comfort, who comforts us in all our affliction, so that we may be able to comfort those who are in any affliction, with the comfort with which we ourselves are comforted by God.

—2 Corinthians 1:3–4

Have you ever noticed that your conversations with someone who has walked a similar path to yours can be particularly riveting? That person understands your journey though few words are shared. As a result, an unusual depth to the relationship sets in quickly. That's what it's like to be understood.

God completely understands what you're going through. He notices your pain and comforts you in it. His comfort touches the depth of your being. He is familiar with all your suffering. He knows exactly how much you are misheard and misunderstood. Those who don't receive his comfort live with wounds in the soul that continue for years. God's comfort is quiet but powerful. He makes the most difficult journey manageable by his comfort.

One of the surprises in this unwanted journey is that you will begin to understand the pain of others like you never did before. Those who have walked a similar path will share with you because you understand, and you have no judgment. They find in you a safe place to be heard. You will become a refuge for them.

As you then receive the comfort Christ has for you, you'll be able to comfort others who lean upon you in a way you never could before. It's as simple as passing on a scripture that God used to steady you amid the drama of the day. You'll find that word of encouragement to be timely more often than not. Whenever God does something, his intentions are broad. He means for us to comfort others with the very same comfort we have received from him.

Our conclusion then must be that there is purpose to the pain. With God, suffering is never pointless. Surrounding you are individuals who agonize quietly over the crushing burden of mental illness, sometimes compounded by addiction. They don't know the comfort of God, but they will—through you.

> Dear Father,
> Thank you for comforting my troubled heart. Though sorrows abound, you bring me peace. You are my strength. Make me mindful of others who are walking a path like mine, whom I might comfort even as you have comforted me. Thank you for bringing purpose to my pain.
> In Jesus's name, amen.

MOVING THE GOAL POSTS
Day Five
Read Matthew 12:18–21

…a bruised reed he will not break, and a smoldering wick he will not quench…

—Matthew 12:20

Normally, a person who moves the goalposts in the middle of a game would be considered a cheater. They're obviously manipulating things to their own advantage. Other times, such as when we're playing with children, we would happily move the goalposts to accommodate a different skill level.

Living alongside a loved one who struggles with mental illness demands the moving of goalposts. Your goal, at least in the immediate, is no longer to get them through college or some career path. The new goal may well be keeping them alive today. Perhaps it is to have them eat three healthy meals and be asleep in their own bed when night comes.

The goalposts must move, at least for now, both for their sake and yours.

Today's reading is from Isaiah, who was looking ahead, anticipating Christ. Jesus's manner is described here as being gentle towards the weak. There are many people who are bruised reeds or smouldering wicks. They're found to the side somewhere, often trying to be invisible. A bruised reed has no strength and would break with the slightest wind, never to recover. A smouldering wick is one that puts out a lot of smoke but is unable to break into flame. Most people would have no patience for either. We would bypass that reed and throw out the lamp. Yet that individual has no less value than the CEO. Jesus isn't affected by the world's shallow definitions of value; each individual is precious to him and he notices them all.

The way forward then is to pray into those immediate goals. What is the need for today? What is the next thing God wants to do in your loved one? Pray that. This isn't to say that the other prayers are irrelevant, but rather that if you have no sense of what God is doing right now in your loved one, you will miss the joy of those smaller victories, and you may unknowingly crush your loved one because you're throwing the ball too far down the field. The goalposts must move.

Dear Father,
Thank you for your patience with human weakness. Have mercy on me and my loved one. Tell me what you wish to do next in my loved one and direct me as I pray. Give me tenderness for my loved one, even as you are tender. Patience and wisdom please, Father!
In Jesus's name, amen.

GOD'S WISDOM IN THE SEA OF CONFUSION
Week Fourteen
Introduction

Do you ever have one of those days when you're in shock over yet another thing that's gone wrong? You wonder how this could possibly be happening. Confusion seems to be part of the everyday equation for the one living alongside someone who struggles with addiction and perhaps mental illness—that and the feeling of being overwhelmed.

I remember sitting at the funeral of a beloved uncle. Our son was with us, though he had to stay back from the funeral itself, nursing a hangover. I was beyond exhausted and overwhelmed. As we sat at the reception, I couldn't stop crying. The sadness of the loss, combined with the long grief I was living through with my son, was more than I could bear.

Life was like trying to cross a fast-moving stream where all the rocks are hidden. They were certainly there; you knew it each time you ran into one. Crossing the stream is challenging and often dangerous. How does one reach the other side? To make matters worse, the river never seems to abate. The water is always high and the current swift. The rocks underneath simply aren't visible. Each day, as it turns out, we need to get to the other side, and there are no bridges in sight. How does one do it?

We need help to get across. We need someone who can keep us from being swept away by the current, someone who can help us navigate the ever-present and hidden rocks. This is the kind of guide we need!

Life demands that we keep living it. In the middle of the confusion, decisions must be made, bills paid, family and friends cared for, and jobs done well. Our loved one having had another bad weekend is not an acceptable excuse to an employer who is looking for our best. The trouble is, this kind of weekend isn't unusual! Yet God is with us and he will help us. He has wisdom for us in the middle of the confusion.

WHY WAIT FOR JOY?

Day One
Read James 1:2–5

Count it all joy, my brothers, when you meet trials of various kinds, for you know that the testing of your faith produces steadfastness. And let steadfastness have its full effect, that you may be perfect and complete, lacking in nothing. If any of you lacks wisdom, let him ask God, who gives generously to all without reproach, and it will be given him.

—James 1:2–5

It seems a bit of a stretch to find joy in our trials. Who in their right mind would willingly choose a path of sorrow like this? If we knew of a convenient way out, would we not take it?

We miss something, though, if all we see is sorrow and we only desire escape. Our own character is shaped by the very trial we walk through. Character is precious to God. He is fashioning something that, if given time, will bring us to spiritual maturity. We feel our lack today at every turn, don't we?

Yet God is bringing us to a place of dependence upon him, to a place in which we will find our satisfaction in him. In this place, we live out of the resources he supplies from heaven. It is a rich place. Here the peace of God sustains us every day. His comfort is palpable. The wisdom of God here is what we live by and rely completely upon.

As we reach out to God, we find him to be what we need. Over time, we learn to do this more and more so that he becomes our life and his presence our greatest joy. When this becomes routine, we aren't sure we want to go back to how things were before, for God has done so much in us.

The key to finding our way through this trial is to ask God for wisdom. He helps us understand the purpose of this difficulty, what he is accomplishing in it and how we should navigate it. Otherwise our suffering seems pointless and we feel on our own, which isn't true. We have assurance that he hears our prayers and guides us into the path of heavenly wisdom.

Dear Father,
Thank you for your unfailing presence. I am out of my depth in this trial and don't know how to understand it or navigate it. Show me the purpose of it. Teach me what you're doing through it. How might I keep step with you in it? Show me where you are that I might fix my eyes on you. Give me your peace today and comfort me by your presence. Watch over my loved one.
In Jesus's name, amen.

THE NON-DESERTER

Day Two

Read Psalm 3

> *...many are saying of my soul, "There is no salvation for him in God." But you, O Lord, are a shield about me, my glory, and the lifter of my head... I lay down and slept; I woke again, for the Lord sustained me.*
> —Psalm 3:2–3, 5

We all have things we need deliverance from. In this psalm, David is surrounded on every side by trouble; even his own son turned against him. To make matters worse, people are talking, saying that his situation is hopeless. They're of the mind that God himself has abandoned him. They're reading between the lines and coming up with what seems like the only logical conclusion to such a desperate plight.

Have you ever been in that spot? Friends close to you look on the intense confusion coming at you through your loved one and they don't mince words: your situation is beyond hope. On top of all the trouble you face, you now have to deal with their words. You are basically done for, they say.

At such times, you must cry out to God. It is wise to put their words out of your mind, and perhaps their influence altogether, and call out to God in your distress. He will deliver you. God always delivers the one who calls out to him. God will lift your head. You are distraught, but in your pain you reach out to him and he hears you, lifting up your head. It matters not how great is the confusion and deep the dysfunction that presents itself. You look to God, for he will save you. He is the only one who can rescue. He is the solid rock on which you must stand in the storm.

Does this mean he's going to stop our loved ones from destroying themselves with drugs or alcohol one painful day after another? Maybe. But more likely he's going to do for you what is needed today. He will feed your soul.

Quite likely, he delivers our loved ones from evil much more than we know. We thankfully don't see our loved ones in the worst of times, but God does.

Sleeping often doesn't come easily to me. I acknowledged my troubles, but they are not a surprise to God. He has seen this day already and will walk with us through it, giving us hope and sleep as we call to him.

Dear Father,
Thank you for never leaving me. Thank you that my situation is never beyond hope. You are my deliverer. Save me from despair and have mercy on my loved one. May your peace fill my heart today. I receive it with thanksgiving.
In Jesus's name, amen.

FIGURING OUT THE MESS
Day Three
Read Colossians 1:15–17

He is the image of the invisible God, the firstborn of all creation. For by him all things were created, in heaven and on earth, visible and invisible, whether thrones or dominions or rulers or authorities—all things were created through him and for him. And he is before all things, and in him all things hold together.
—Colossians 1:15–17

I enjoy crocheting, but sometimes the ball of yarn gets so tangled up that I cannot keep working on my project until I stop and get all the knots out! Sometimes it takes a while. How many times do we find our days are like that? Only in this case we have no idea how to untangle the challenges we're in.

I find comfort and a measure of peace in these words: *"he is before all things, and in him all things hold together"* (Colossians 1:17). There are certain things I can sort out when I apply myself. However, many things are beyond me. This is particularly the case when what needs sorting out has to do with another person. In these situations, there are many loose ends entirely beyond our control. We need God to sort it out.

It's not just that Jesus is the glue that holds all things together; he is also the end to which they all move. As today's passage reminds us, all things were created through him and for him. The problem comes when people don't have this as their goal: to live for Christ. It puts people out of sync with what God made us for. That's when confusion comes, because we're serving a different purpose than what he intended for us.

His blessing comes when we align ourselves with him. Outside of that, we begin to experience increasing disorder. Only God knows the way back from that dark place. Only he can awaken a heart to be aware that they are even in a dark place and then come to a point of conviction from which he will help them find their way back home.

We don't need to be anxious as we pray about these situations. Remember, God's got this and he will sort it out, even though we don't know when or how. Choose to trust him.

Dear Father,
Thank you for holding everything together. Thank you for having sorted out my life. As I give you the rest of the tangles and mess, you will take care of them as well. I trust you with all of it. Fill my heart with peace that comes from you.
In Jesus's name, amen.

ORDER OUT OF CHAOS
Day Four
Read Psalm 46:10, Isaiah 41:10

Be still, and know that I am God. I will be exalted among the nations, I will be exalted in the earth!
—Psalm 46:10

...fear not, for I am with you; be not dismayed, for I am your God; I will strengthen you, I will help you, I will uphold you with my righteous right hand.
—Isaiah 41:10

Today is a good day to read these promises from God. Are you anxious and fearful of where things might go? Does stillness escape you, having been replaced by exhaustion? Does it feel like the whims and ambitions of another rule the day, leaving you to feel like a helpless pawn?

Such is the making of confusion. In the midst of it, though, God still reigns and will be exalted in our situations as we look to him. We often don't understand how that could possibly come about, nor are we entitled to know it. We can, however, simply trust God.

God alone takes what is chaotic and brings order. No one else can do that. It's tempting to want to control or overthink what is before us, but we need not do that. Even when others are intent on exalting themselves, God is able to bring about his purposes. Confusion need not win the day for the one who looks to him. Trust God in the mist of confusion.

Amid all that God does in this process, he doesn't forget you. You will find his comfort and strength in the disorder. Dismay slips to the side with the growing awareness that God holds your hand and guides you.

How many days I thought about these simple truths the morning after my loved one spent most of the night drinking. Sleep was hard to come by, but this knowledge—that God is still God in the middle of the disappointments and is with me—brought me comfort.

Take a moment to stop your racing mind and reflect on this: God is sovereign over all and he is with you.

Dear Father,
I quiet myself in your presence. Forgive me for my anxiety and fear; I lose sight of you easily. Bring order out of the confusion that I find myself in and seems to run over me. I invite you to bring your purposes to bear in it and your name to be lifted up. Thank you for your presence and your help. I turn away from dismay and rest in your love. Save my loved one.
In Jesus's name, amen.

MANAGE YOUR GAZE
Day Five
Read Matthew 14:22–36

But immediately Jesus spoke to them, saying, "Take heart; it is I. Do not be afraid."

—Matthew 14:27

It's the middle of the night and the disciples have been at the oars for hours. Everyone is exhausted. Where should we fix our gaze when all we have are wind and waves, with little progress being made?

Their fear abated when they heard the voice of Jesus, *"Take heart; it is I. Do not be afraid"* (Matthew 14:27).

First, remember that Jesus sends us into storms… but he intends from the outset to get us to the other side. The storm doesn't jeopardize the outcome.

Second, remember that his eye is upon us constantly. He is never far away.

Third, finding our way through the storm is exhausting. It hits when you're tired and your resources are spent.

Fourth, the storm is not overwhelming to you; Christ walks on it effortlessly.

Fifth, he reveals himself to you in the storm. In that moment, you become oblivious to the wind and waves. You will learn things of Christ in the middle of storms you will never discover sitting on a beach.

Sixth, when he speaks peace to you, it is not a mild suggestion. It is a work of power that immediately quiets your spirit.

Seeing this, Peter asked to likewise walk on the water. As Jesus invited him, Peter stepped out of the boat. Interestingly, the storm raged on, but only when Peter took his eyes off Jesus did he notice afresh the terrible waves. Fear took over and Jesus had to rescue him from drowning.

When you love someone struggling with addictions, great storms make the journey difficult. Fear is common. Yet Jesus invites you to walk through the storm as he does. This is not a gift that comes by hard work or even by practice. You must look to him in simple trust. If you sink, he will rescue you. Maybe next time you'll keep your eyes on him and let the storm rage.

Dear Father,
Thank you for noticing me in this sea of confusion and coming to me. Reveal yourself to me to still my anxious heart. Call me to walk through the storm as you do. Teach me to keep my eyes fixed on you. Rescue me when I fall. Thank you for your unfailing love.
In Jesus's name, amen.

PUTTING ANGER IN ITS PLACE
Week Fifteen
Introduction

When I think of anger, it reminds me of times when I've burned soup while cooking. Though the burnt part is limited to the bottom of the pot, stuck firmly there, it taints the entire batch. That pungent taste is in every mouthful. Try as I might, I cannot escape it. Even if I add other spices, they pale in comparison to the lingering burnt flavour.

When anger quietly brews in our souls, it has a way of expressing itself. It cannot remain hidden without infecting the rest of our being.

One of the great challenges in walking with a loved one who is addicted or struggling with mental illness is keeping your own anger in its place. Broken promises, things stolen, and hurtful words all build up to wear down trust and leave you feeling increasingly angry. What should be done with that anger?

When I was a child, my father, while drunk, gave away one of my Christmas gifts. I didn't receive many gifts, so the loss of this one, which I had most wished for, was heart-breaking for me. I was angry for a long time. In such situations, we must live with the consequences of the drunken choices of those we love and there is nothing easy about that.

This week, we will take time to consider what God has to say to us about our anger. We cannot deny what we feel. Though it may feel justified, do we really want this emotion to control us as it has? Let's consider God's word together.

QUICK TO HEAR

Day One
Read James 1:19–20

…let every person be quick to hear, slow to speak, slow to anger; for the anger of man does not produce the righteousness of God.

—James 1:19–20

The choice to listen intently to people, careful to hear them as they wish to be understood, isn't common. We often feel misunderstood and, too frequently, we misunderstand. It's easy to jump to conclusions and make hasty judgments.

This is particularly true when communicating with a loved one who is addicted. Because of the recurring patterns, we come to conclusions quickly. We're somewhat wearied by the excuses and stories. Our mistrust comes through loud and clear, which only makes the situation worse. The unwillingness to listen carefully betrays our impatience and often our growing anger.

Anger, however, must be watched carefully and given fences to contain it or it spreads. It keeps a person from listening well. The angry person cannot hear. Their ears become blocked by hurt and often a deep sense of injustice.

One of the things that will help us to hear is asking God to speak to us about our loved one. Maybe we're missing something. Listen for what he wants to say about your loved one. He may show why they're doing what they do. Perhaps he'll reveal to you their fear or insecurity. God will help you to see your loved one in a different light, and when he does you'll have greater empathy and probably less anger. You will need to become quiet, though, to hear him.

We need an anchor to hold us steady amid the strong emotions we feel. As I read this passage, the image of a boat anchored in the middle of a lake comes to mind. That boat might drift a bit as the waves and wind move it around, but it's not going anywhere. The anchor holds it secure.

God's word at work in us has the same effect. Remember this verse today. It will anchor you and save you from regret or further strain on your relationship. It will remind you to never stop listening and to think before you respond, allowing wisdom to rise as we stop, listen, and pray.

Dear Father,
Regardless of what I may hear today, help me to listen carefully and respond with wisdom. Forgive me for allowing anger to control me. It is never far from me as I see and hear things that disappoint me. Live your life in me. Give me your patience and understanding. Help me see my loved one differently. Heal my raw emotions. Have mercy on my loved one, and have mercy on me.
In Jesus's name, amen.

SLOW TO BECOME ANGRY

Day Two

Read Proverbs 29:11

A fool gives full vent to his spirit, but a wise man quietly holds it back.

—Proverbs 29:11

There is a game young people play with a tube of toothpaste. First they squeeze out all the toothpaste, and then they must put it back. This game is often used to demonstrate that it's impossible to take back words that are carelessly spoken.

When we express ourselves in anger, we will likely regret what we say. Even if it's true, it may not be wise. Just because something is true doesn't mean it should be spoken.

These volatile situations call for wisdom, which is consistently marked by self-restraint. The urge to speak freely in such moments is strong. Everything in us wants to speak up and set this person straight once and for all. When we blow our top, it's not helpful and often damages people. Relationships that were imperfect but still growing now become stalled.

It may help us to consider that our anger is seldom perfect. We may be reacting to our own fears and insecurities. Maybe our loved one is hitting some old, familiar buttons that when pushed throw us off our resolve and cause us to fly off the handle. Perhaps we're being faced with some of our own failures or weaknesses of character.

Much as we feel justified in our anger, it is seldom righteous. Our anger is tainted with our imperfections, and as a result it's unhelpful. We may also believe that saying what we really think will make us feel better, but that is often not the case.

Another way to hold back is to stop speaking about the situation that grieves you so deeply. The more you talk about your disappointment and frustration, the angrier you become. There comes a time when we realize that we've talked enough about it.

One key then is to trust God. If your loved one is hitting buttons, yield those buttons to God and let him heal your heart. Let him sort out these troubling situations. Walk under his instruction as you consider your loved one.

Dear Father,
Would you soothe my strong emotions? My anger is so unprofitable. Forgive me for foolish things I have said in my wrath. Heal me and strengthen what is weak. Would you intervene and rescue my loved one from their folly? I am at the end of all my solutions. Teach me what I should do.
In Jesus's name, amen.

PURSUE WORDS OF HEALING
Day Three
Read Proverbs 12:18

There is one whose rash words are like sword thrusts, but the tongue of the wise brings healing.
—Proverbs 12:18

If a relationship in our lives requires extra attention, it's the one we have with our loved one who struggles. Today's short verse from Proverbs is like a well-packed suitcase. There are few words, yet it teaches us much on how to respond to the angry and often hurtful words of a loved one.

First, we are wise to recognize the conversation for what it is. The chances of this loved one remembering what they said in a drunken outburst the next day are very low.

Second, though the conversation may not be remembered by your loved one, the words they spoke were terrible and are emblazoned in your memory. Their words were like sword thrusts, each jab delivered in anger and cruelty. Your loved one may move on easily with the day, but you'll be left crumpled emotionally because of the pain of those hurtful words. They were not neutral words; at the time, they were meant to harm. The only way to escape their dark power is to forgive.

Third, our words in response don't have to be in like manner. Rather, we may speak in such a way that brings healing. Our words can heal by not adding fuel to the fire, by not taking the bait from leading questions and sharp accusations. Simply choosing to not get involved already diffuses the anger. It's difficult to fight when only one side is throwing the punches.

Since healing words have their source in God, ask him for them. Anger is common, but healing is uncommon. We feel our dependence greatly at such times, but as we lean on God, he gives us words and thoughts that may surprise us.

Also, as we immerse ourselves in the word of God, he will help us get past our own anger and teach us a way of wisdom that has its source in heaven. Remember, God's ways are very different from ours.

Dear Father,
Your thoughts are much higher than mine. Teach me yours. I want to walk in them. Heal my heart so that I will not respond out of my own pain in these intense situations. I feel my need of you so desperately. Give me healing words for all my conversations. Thank you for your presence and wisdom, no matter how messy this day may become.
In Jesus's name, amen.

THERE'S MORE AT STAKE THAN YOU THINK
Day Four
Read Ephesians 4:26–27

Be angry and do not sin; do not let the sun go down on your anger, and give no opportunity to the devil.
—Ephesians 4:26–27

When anger lingers, there is much at stake. We feel entitled to our anger because of the injustice of the situation and the insensitivity of the comments made. However, we don't realize that the enemy of our soul is looking to find an even more significant point of entrance into the family.

When he speaks through our loved ones who are under the influence of some substance, having thus opened a door to his dark presence, that is a terrible thing. Those words are cold and mean-spirited every time.

They are, however, still outside of us: they are just words. We can dismiss them, knowing that our loved ones aren't themselves in such moments.

Alternatively, we may choose to linger on them, brooding over the insensitivity. The longer we stew on how unfair the whole situation is, the angrier we become. At the end of the day, our unchecked bitterness grows into lingering anger, and the enemy finds an opportunity not only with our loved one, but also with us. We give the devil opportunity to bring untold confusion into our homes by our own anger. This is exactly what he wants.

We will have no joy, no peace, and no love in this state. That place is dark and the enemy is in charge. When we think it can get no worse, it does! It will continue this way until we forgive our loved one and repent of our anger.

Though we may feel we have every right to be angry, we are wise to guard our hearts from all bitterness regardless of the source. Bitterness and anger never serve to help us. They are like poison that colours how we see our loved ones in their struggles. We are only hurting ourselves and being robbed of peace.

Give this situation to God in all its unkindness, heartbreak, and disappointment. Leave it with him to sort out what you cannot. Then give thanks for whatever you are able, however small it may seem.

Dear Father,
I confess to you how angry I feel some days. Deliver me from a spirit of anger. I ask that you would comfort me. Drain the anger out of me. Take this difficult situation and sort it out. There is so little in it that pleases you, yet I want to please you with my life. Thank you for helping me to forgive… again. Thank you for all the good that is still around me.
In Jesus's name, amen.

CHOOSE GENTLENESS
Day Five
Read Proverbs 15:1, Proverbs 19:11

A soft answer turns away wrath, but a harsh word stirs up anger.

—Proverbs 15:1

Good sense makes one slow to anger, and it is his glory to overlook an offense.

—Proverbs 19:11

You cannot love someone who is struggling with addiction without having to overlook a lot. How we respond still matters. Anger breeds anger, just as kindness breeds kindness. An argument only continues because we allow it to. It takes two to argue. As soon as one drops out, the dispute loses its strength. How is a gentle answer even possible given the hostility of many of these situations?

First, recognize that gentleness is a fruit of the Spirit (Galatians 5:22–23). It is a quality which God produces as we yield to him. It is God living his life in you. He is gentle. He is very different from us. But when we prayerfully linger in his word, he forms gentleness in us even in the most hostile situations. Gentleness is not natural to us in these situations. Only the Lord Jesus can be gentle in these scenarios. Confess your need to him and lean heavily upon him and you will find the same quality growing in you.

Second, remember that God has been gracious to you, as have other people no doubt. We all need mercy. You cannot take all your loved one's words seriously or they will crush you. Overlook them even as others have overlooked some of your own careless words. And take some time to thank God for his great mercy, which doesn't treat us as we deserve.

Third, though it may feel like we are enabling their misbehaviour, they need to own it, even though they are being driven by compulsion. Much of their anger is misdirected. They're often upset with themselves for their own failures. They know that they aren't doing well. As a result, they seek to blame someone, and sadly the ones they love are often the target.

It is wise to not give them grounds for their outbursts. A gentle answer will leave them to face themselves squarely, which is what they most need.

Dear Father,
Thank you for overlooking the foolish things I have said and done. Have mercy on me. Keep me from harsh replies to my loved one. Forgive me for the many times I have said what I should not have and acted in ways that were not honourable. Fill me with your Spirit so that I might walk a different path. Form gentleness in me.
In Jesus's name, amen.

OVERCOMING EVIL
Week Sixteen
Introduction

My brother already struggled with alcoholism in his early teens. When he was older, he began to mix his drinking with drugs. It was this practice that caused his first cardiac arrest. As we sat in the hospital ICU, we prayed with him and over him many times. He wasn't expected to live… but he did.

He had a second cardiac arrest days later. We were called in once again.

My brother was lying on the hospital bed, his shirt open with the paddles they'd used to restart his heart sitting on his chest ready, just in case. I stood by his bed and silently prayed the peace of Christ over him as I gently stroked his arm.

He spoke to me directly. "What are you doing?"

I told him that I was just rubbing your arm.

"No!" he said again. "What are you doing?"

I explained that I was praying for him.

"When you do that, you make all the voices stop."

I was shocked when he told me that. I hadn't known there were voices speaking to him. How had they gotten there, I wondered? What had given them the right to torment my brother?

We prayed earnestly for my brother over the few years that followed until his death. He never did experience freedom from the drugs, sadly, but he did seek God in his way. He did his best to come to church—although because of the drugs he took, he slept through much of it.

The last time I saw my brother alive, he was sitting in church. Getting there was a massive effort for him.

I wish this story had a happier ending, but it does not.

One might assume that nothing like this could ever befall your loved one. The evil one dwells in all the places your loved one goes to drink, do drugs, and become intoxicated. Evil goes where sin is celebrated and embraced. Our loved ones open doors to their souls for evil simply by their behaviour.

In this next week, we want to focus on how to overcome the powers of evil and not be afraid. When Jesus died for us, he overcame the powers of evil. We live out of that victory. It's helpful for us to speak openly about this. May God fill your heart with his peace and much courage as we look into this. We have nothing to fear.

JESUS, GREATER THAN ALL

Day One

Read Philippians 2:5–11

…he humbled himself by becoming obedient to the point of death, even death on a cross. Therefore God has highly exalted him and bestowed on him the name that is above every name…

—Philippians 2:8–9

There is none like Jesus. The story of him humbling himself and dying in our place will never stop being told, even in heaven. Because of his obedience in self-sacrificial death, he was lifted up and given authority over everything in heaven and on earth. When we consider our struggles with evil in this world, this is where we must begin. All evil is under his feet.

Our loved ones sadly open the way for this darkness to afflict them through their addiction/behaviour. To be under the control of some substance is to no longer be in control of ourselves and then to open a door for evil spirits to control us. Though this isn't always the case, it often is. The state of a person in such a condition becomes decidedly worse.

However, there is always a way out of the darkest and most hopeless places of confinement. It has to do with Jesus. He is greater than all and is able to save anyone who looks to him. This is where we find hope and solid ground in an evil day. He can dismiss any evil forces, for he has defeated them on the cross. They tremble before him and listen to him, as they do to us, for we are in him. The way forward then is to lift Jesus up in our prayers, because he is greater than all.

Do not fear evil; trust in God and humble yourself before him. Evil spirits are always proud. They have nothing in common with humility and are powerless before it. Though it seems to us so weak, humility is a mighty weapon against dark forces. Go low before God. Confess your sins to him. Become obedient to God on the things he has been speaking to you about and give thanks to him. How can evil stand before such a person?

Dear Father,
I praise you, for you are greater than all. Thank you for overcoming evil on the cross. Thank you for saving me from the evil one. Forgive my sins. I turn away from pride and self-interest. I am here to do your will. Deliver me from all fear of evil and fill me instead with the vision of your greatness. Set my loved one free from all evil.
In Jesus's name, amen.

THE LOVE AND POWER OF JESUS
Day Two
Read Luke 8:26–38

Then people went out to see what had happened, and they came to Jesus and found the man from whom the demons had gone, sitting at the feet of Jesus, clothed and in his right mind, and they were afraid.

—Luke 8:35

In this story, we catch a glimpse of the heart of God. Jesus demonstrates his belief that this man who hadn't been to anyone's house for dinner in a long time was worth the trip across the lake. Evidently, he went all that way to help this one man, for he left immediately afterward.

Jesus came to set captives free. He doesn't view anyone in bondage as a lost cause or waste of time. He loved this troubled man just as he does your loved one.

Recognizing the presence of evil is helpful for us as we relate to our loved ones. We see some of its marks in this story. A person affected by evil spirits increasingly lives alone, self-isolating and being isolated by others. Self-harm is often present in their life such that their relentless self-destruction mystifies us. These individuals feel powerless at times in the grip of what controls them to do shameful things.

Also, evil spirits can express themselves through a person's voice, which explains why your loved one's words can be so cutting at times. Most importantly, they recognize Jesus and fear him utterly.

Though evil wreaks havoc in the lives of our loved ones, Jesus is neither shocked nor intimidated by the scene and doesn't run from it. He has come to set our loved ones free. He has come to give life to your loved one, no matter how troubled they are. Reach out to him in prayer. Present your loved one to God in the name of Jesus.

The end result is striking. This man who had lived naked among the tombs now sits clothed at the feet of Jesus, in his right mind. That is the effect of Jesus. We are comforted to know that regardless of how terrible the place where our loved ones might be, Jesus has his eyes on them and comes, even now, to set them free, if they are willing.

Dear Father,
Thank you for your love for every shattered life. I praise you, for you are not afraid of dark and deserted spaces. Visit our family and release every captive here. Drive out the darkness and break each chain. Bring in a fresh experience in your lovingkindness. Lead my loved one to spiritual freedom.
In Jesus's name, amen.

BREAKING STRONGHOLDS
Day Three
Read 2 Corinthians 10:3–5

For though we walk in the flesh, we are not waging war according to the flesh. For the weapons of our warfare are not of the flesh but have divine power to destroy strongholds. We destroy arguments and every lofty opinion raised against the knowledge of God...

—2 Corinthians 10:3–5

War is ugly and it's of the utmost importance to wield weapons which will prove effective against the enemy. Scripture teaches that we are in a spiritual conflict in regard to our loved ones, and we are up against evil strongholds. These are firmly entrenched behaviours and systems of thought that seem unbreakable though they are contrary to the will of God. These belief systems have pride at their root, for they are lifted up against the knowledge of God. They seem to laugh at us. As a result, we can be filled with hopelessness as they mockingly say they will never yield.

However, we destroy those very strongholds. We do this by God's methods and the weapons which bear his power.

First, we hold to what he teaches in his word, not what presents itself to our eyes. Regardless of what behaviour is manifested against us, we cling to what God says and do not yield in our hearts to hopelessness.

Second, we pray the truth of the word of God into the situation in two directions. We dismantle each prideful thought that stands against God in the life and behaviour of our loved one, one at a time, by identifying it and simply saying no in the mighty name of Jesus.

Next we bind what is false and tormenting. Then we pray what the Scriptures say is true about our loved one, all of God's good purposes and ways. All of this happens in the quietness of our own prayer rooms.

Write out Bible verses key to your situation and pray them daily in this manner. Though you cannot change your loved one's heart, you can demolish these strongholds. Your prayers will make a difference with your loved one.

Dear Father,
Thank you that evil strongholds must yield to prayers that flow from your word. Give me discernment that I might understand the lies and half-truths that bind my loved one. I take my stand against all evil strongholds. Let them all come down. Then release all your good purposes for my loved one, all that is good, right, and true.
In Jesus's name, amen.

THE VALUE OF SMALL FAITH
Day Four
Read Mark 9:14–29

But if you can do anything, have compassion on us and help us." And Jesus said to him, "'If you can'! All things are possible for one who believes." Immediately the father of the child cried out and said, "I believe; help my unbelief!"

—Mark 9:22–24

Who of us would say we have great faith? Having a loved one mired in addiction over a prolonged period of time tends to make one's claim to faith humbler. Fortunately, Jesus lifted up the importance of even small faith.

In this story, a broken-hearted father came to Jesus seeking healing for his son, who was demonized. The symptoms are chilling, and we wonder how one's condition could become so dreadful. The callous nature of evil troubles us, but more importantly, like this father, it stirs us to action and we begin to cry out in desperation to God.

What surprises us perhaps is the role of faith in the healing of our loved ones. Do you struggle, like the father, to believe that Jesus is able to set your loved one free? Jesus does not bypass the issue. Though he's able to do anything, Jesus hesitated in this case, even while the boy was convulsing on the ground, and talked to the father about where his faith was at.

We like to think that we are passive in the whole process of healing. Jesus sees things differently. It is essential that we ask, trust, and thank him for the healing of our loved ones. We are in a partnership with God on the things we wait on him for.

A different issue, also of faith, rises with the disciples. They believed but were unable to see any change come to the boy's condition. Do you feel that? Jesus says it is because of a lack of prayer.

Faith is dependence on God. Our flawed faith shows up when we lose heart or act like we have something to prove. Rather, we pray for our loved one and wait on God for his instructions. Desperation and panic move to the sidelines as a quiet confidence in God settles upon us, and out of that we pray with faith. The evil one must relinquish his place in the face of prevailing prayer.

Dear Father,
Forgive me for taking my eyes off you. You alone heal and set my loved one free from long-standing chains. I look to you and wait upon you. I present my loved one to you in the name of Jesus. Thank you for overcoming evil on the cross. Manifest that victory now in my loved one.
In Jesus's name, amen.

BECOMING BATTLE READY
Day Five
Read Ephesians 6:10–18

Finally, be strong in the Lord and in the strength of his might. Put on the whole armor of God, that you may be able to stand against the schemes of the devil.

—Ephesians 6:10–11

Whether or not we want to be involved in spiritual warfare, we are. God means for each one of us to take a stand against evil spirits and their plans for our loved ones. This means, of course, that we are able to do this. The key is to be strong in the Lord, putting on the specific spiritual armour he has given us.

First, we put on the belt of truth, because we need discernment to recognize the subtle lies, half-truths, and deceiving ways of Satan.

Second, in putting on the breastplate of righteousness, we choose the path of righteousness. It is unrighteous living that opens the door for the evil one.

Third, we put on shoes that are made ready with the gospel of peace. True peace that guards our hearts comes from God. It is this peace we carry with us everywhere we go.

Fourth, as we take up the shield of faith, we have a defence against the flaming arrows which are hurled at us. Count on Christ to protect you from these cruel arrows of the enemy so that he might not hurt you or keep you from doing God's will in regard to your loved one.

Fifth, the mind is protected with the helmet of salvation because there is a battle for your thoughts. We need protection from dark and hopeless thoughts. Ask for the mind of Christ.

Finally, the sword of the Spirit is the word of God. We immerse ourselves in it and use it against the lies of the enemy. It is a mighty sword and a springboard for our best prayers. Read the Scriptures back to God as you pray for your loved one, claiming its promises and reclaiming any ground that was lost.

Dealing with evil doesn't require an expert; it requires someone who knows they belong to God and are ready to stand and fight in the mighty name of Jesus.

Dear Father,
Thank you for the provision you have given me for this spiritual conflict. Thank you for the reminder that my loved one is not the enemy. Today I put on the Lord Jesus. He is my protection in each of these ways. Make me strong in him and in his mighty power. I choose the way of prayer and will live in that place of thankful dependence upon you.
In Jesus's name, amen.

A LONG WAIT IN THE RIGHT DIRECTION
Week Seventeen
Introduction

Who doesn't enjoy a pleasant journey which is fun and just long enough? However, other journeys are preferably over quickly, such as childbirth. Though it's rough, you know that a baby will indeed be born—hopefully sooner than later!

If only this journey with our loved one would be like that! If there were some magic way in which we could abbreviate it and move today to the road of recovery, we would. That power, sadly, is not given to us. This journey will take as long as it will take. Not only are we without the power to shorten the journey, there is no rule of thumb to predict its duration. We feel our limitations deeply as we care for our loved ones.

What we do know is that when the day finally arrives, there will be a great deal of thanksgiving. Celebrating one year sober was deeply significant for our son, as it was for us. He is now five years sober. Not one day goes by that we don't thank God for what our son's life is today. The thanksgiving continues to fill our hearts.

Staying the course over a long period of time is essential for this unwanted journey we find ourselves on. We desperately need the Good Shepherd to steady us. This week, let's consider how we might become better equipped and encouraged for a journey that takes far too long.

TROUBLESHOOTING EXHAUSTION

Day One

Read Psalm 6

My soul also is greatly troubled. But you, O Lord—how long? …I am weary with my moaning; every night I flood my bed with tears; I drench my couch with my weeping.

—Psalm 6:3, 6

Long waits are seldom fun. If you've waited for people to arrive on a plane that has been delayed, cancelled, and rebooked, you know. When your people finally arrive, you are full of joy!

This is how it is when we come to God with our broken hearts. He hears the anguish of our soul and delights in our prayers. However, we get tripped up sometimes and as a result find ourselves deeply wearied.

We get stuck on the many reasons God might be upset with us. We all have regrets, such as how we responded to our loved one, and accepting forgiveness can be a struggle. The psalmist gets past that (Psalm 6:1–3). God sees past our failures. When we get stuck there, we fail to see the greatness of his mercy and his eagerness to heal us.

The second thing that inhibits our endurance is that we are calling out to God for our own sakes. We have so much pain. How could it be otherwise? There is, however, a higher form of prayer. The psalmist learned to pray for God's sake, to see his own concerns through God's eyes (Psalm 6:4–5). When you see your loved one through God's eyes, it lends considerable strength and courage to your prayers. God gave you this loved one with a definite purpose.

The third way in which we get tripped up is to stay in our grief without ever coming to a place of rest in the grace of God, who has definitely heard us (Psalm 6:6–10). When we stay in grief because of our loved one, we wear ourselves out. Even though our situation remains unchanged, God gives us peace and assurance that he will do good. Faith rises in the place of long suffering so that we will know he has heard us and we can trust him with the outcome. Peace then seeps in like sunshine through dark clouds after a long rainy day.

Dear Father,
Thank you for your mercy to me. Thank you for receiving me, though I have done things that haven't been helpful where my loved one is concerned. I present them before you in the name of Jesus and pray that his purposes would be established in their life. For today, though this journey is exhausting, give me your peace in my inmost being. Help me experience your comfort.
In Jesus's name, amen.

THE VALUE OF GAZING UPON BEAUTY

Day Two

Read Psalm 18:31–36

For who is God, but the Lord? And who is a rock, except our God?—the God who equipped me with strength and made my way blameless. He made my feet like the feet of a deer and set me secure on the heights.
—Psalm 18:31–33

If you've ever hiked up a mountain, you know that the pathway can become narrow and steep. The climb can be intense right to the top. However, as you trudge up the difficult incline, you can take time to pause and enjoy the breath-taking scenery which makes the climb more bearable.

The journey with our loved one is undoubtedly difficult and unusually long. The question then is where one finds beauty that would lighten our steps. Sometimes we need God to shine a light for us, so we can see this beauty. It is real.

The psalmist found it in the person and work of God. God is always beautiful. All earthly beauty is but a shadow of him who is perfect in beauty. Every aspect of his character is perfect. His ways are perfect. He is present in our darkest day and to pause and look upon him is to find joy and deepest relief. In such a moment, we make him the centre of our lives again, not our loved one. God is our rock.

His works are stunning as well. In particular, reflect on how he equips you for the very climb you are on. Though the climb is challenging, he gives you strength daily. In this very moment, he makes your way blameless, forgiving and helping you to walk with self-control and wisdom in a volatile situation. He enables you to climb the very heights you walk. If he didn't do this, you would not be there. Like all others, you would be far down the mountainside.

Though we walk such a narrow path fraught with danger, he makes our feet secure. All these are his works and expressions of his majesty.

Dear Father,
I delight in you and look to you. As I reflect on all your perfections, my heart is lightened. When I consider you, this unwanted journey doesn't actually seem so lonely. Thank you for all the ways in which you equip me for this climb. Your provision for me is exactly what I need and entirely a gift from heaven. Thank you for your provision. Thank you for your presence and for remembering me.
In Jesus's name, amen.

FINDING STRENGTH IN THE JOURNEY OF OTHERS
Day Three
Read Psalm 22

My God, my God, why have you forsaken me? ...In you our fathers trusted; they trusted, and you delivered them. To you they cried and were rescued; in you they trusted and were not put to shame.

—Psalm 22:1, 4–5

Prayer is a place of honesty. There we open our hearts to God, even in disappointment. At first it seems almost disrespectful to speak to God of forsaking us. Yet prayer is meant to be the transparent outpouring of the heart.

We feel a number of strong emotions in this unwanted journey. God desires an honest and transparent relationship with us. He invites even our lament. Remember, though, that the lament is towards God and an expression of relationship with him. It is not undirected complaining.

In your lament, remember the others who have known suffering like yours. Rehearse what affliction fell upon them and how it affected them. Consider how long their journey was. Remember how they cried out to God in their suffering, and maybe still do. As they cried out to him, what did he do for them? How did he come to their aid?

Their story is not meant to bring resentment to you, since it has perhaps ended happily while yours hasn't. Rather, it is meant to inspire faith to reach out to God, knowing that he is faithful and hears your prayers as he did theirs.

Like the psalmist, we fear being put to shame and are reluctant to hope. Will he truly come through if we trust in him? The testimonies of others whom God helped, each in their own unwanted journey, are meant to encourage and strengthen us. A breath of fresh air will come to you as you consider the experience of others and how God helped them.

As we press into our times of prayer, give thanks to God for what he has done for other people and then ask him to do the same for you. Never give up. Your loved one is worth fighting for, and so is your sanity! Find your hope in God and cry out honestly to him.

Dear Father,
Thank you for all that you have done in my friends' life. Thank you for your intervention in an impossible situation in response to their prayers. Do it again, Lord. Do it for the glory of your name. I feel tired and weary asking the same thing again and again. I am thankful, though, that you hear me and that I will not be put to shame in my confidence in you. Do the impossible.
In Jesus's name, amen.

LIVING FOR AN ETERNAL REWARD

Day Four

Read James 1:12

Blessed is the man who remains steadfast under trial, for when he has stood the test he will receive the crown of life, which God has promised to those who love him.

—James 1:12

It's probably not true to say we're never motivated by rewards. This was real for us as children and is likely still true! God speaks often of rewards that will be given to those who are faithful to him. He means for these rewards to be significant motivators for his children who follow him, often on difficult pathways. These rewards will be given when we stand before him.

Without minimizing what God gives us now, the Scriptures speak often about eternal rewards. God knew that your journey would be difficult and fraught with setbacks. There would be suffering and disappointments. The journey itself offers little reward. Looking to your loved one for encouragement is often a vain hope. Even what we experience of the presence of God pales in comparison to what God promises us one day. He means to completely fill your heart with hope so that you will be forward-looking all of your days, despite current difficulties.

In this case, God promises a reward for you one day because you persevered under trial. Though your loved one may have misunderstood you, turned against you, and broken your heart, you continued to trust God. No matter how uncertain the outcome, you were faithful to God. You survived one day at a time looking to him for insight. He encouraged you in the midst of it and strengthened you step by step. God wants you to know that he rewards your perseverance through this unwanted journey.

God will reward. He will give you a crown of life because you endured. This world may bring you some encouragement in regard to your loved one. But even if it doesn't, God will definitely reward you. There is so much more in store for you than simply seeing your loved one come around. God will reward you for your faithfulness to him. He sees every sacrifice made. He hears every prayer and sees your growing and tenacious faith. Live for the reward God will give.

Dear Father,
You are life to me. Though I couldn't imagine turning my back on my loved one, thank you for the promise you give to those who persevere. Help me to persevere! Grow my character through this challenge so that my loved one might see Jesus in me. Give me a clearer glimpse of eternity and of eternal reward. Fill me with hope.
In Jesus's name, amen.

FINDING CONTENTMENT
Day Five
Read Psalm 131:1–2

O Lord, my heart is not lifted up; my eyes are not raised too high; I do not occupy myself with things too great and too marvelous for me. But I have calmed and quieted my soul, like a weaned child with its mother; like a weaned child is my soul within me.

—Psalm 131:1–2

Seldom do we understand what goes on beyond the obvious. Our insight in regard to our loved ones and why they do what they do is lacking at almost every turn. We're limited both in understanding and power. Neither do we know the future, though our fears would tell us otherwise.

Relief comes in acknowledging our significant limitations. It helps us remember that we are not God. His understanding is perfect, and as we wait upon him he gives us what we need. The truth is that we are entirely dependent on God. When we wander from that, the way seems long and hard. Allow God to do what only he can.

Instead of grasping too high for things not given to us, we are wise to quiet our anxious souls and find contentment with God, even now.

Today's verse paints the picture of a weaned child with its mother. That child simply leans against its mother and is quiet, no longer clamouring for mother's milk.

We wonder, though, how quietness and contentment is possible in this state of disruption. We argue that contentment will come only when our loved ones leave behind their addictive behaviour and become again the people we once knew.

The contentment of the weaned child lies in knowing who its mother is and finding safety there. Can you not rest in the love of God who is present to you in this moment? Will he not help you and be to you all the wisdom you need? Yes, he will. Do you need to know all the complexities that tomorrow may bring? No, you don't.

Even in the disruption, we are invited to experience this stillness with God. We rest with him and trust him with all the loose ends. His hand is big enough to hold them all. In this, we find peace to carry us through the day.

Dear Father,
You alone are God. Forgive me for grasping too high for things that belong to you alone. Give me insight for the things I need to understand concerning my loved one. Show me the way I should go. Reveal yourself to my loved one and intervene in their life. I quiet myself in your presence knowing that you are trustworthy. I am safe with you.
In Jesus's name, amen.

WOUND CARE FOR TOXIC CONVERSATIONS
Week Eighteen
Introduction

It's highly unlikely that you'll walk with a loved one experiencing addiction and not have memories of toxic text messages or conversations. Sadly, it comes with the territory. A common children's rhyme ends with the assurance that "words will never hurt me." This unfortunately is not the case. Toxic wounds and disappointment can be devastating.

It can be staggering how forgetful our loved ones are of the kindness that has been extended to them, particularly when they're under the influence of some substance. A person's reality is what they see. Responding with wisdom to these conversations and then actually getting past them is no small feat, especially when they keep coming.

On one particularly dark night, my husband and I asked our son to leave. We had found him an alternate place to stay. The text messages that came through the night were scathing and hurtful. There was nothing we could say or do to address the problem in that moment. God brought us comfort; we knew that only he could soothe the deep hurt.

Regardless, we still must deal with what we heard or read, for we cannot unhear it, nor can we unread it. We learned not to rehearse those conversations. When one of us would share what was said, we would do it in very broad terms. Why should we both have to unhear what should never have been spoken?

This week, we will talk about wound care for these conversations that befall us. Let's look to God to put a new song in our mouths. His song breathes new life and hope. Who doesn't need that?

THE ANATOMY OF TOXIC WORDS
Day One
Read Psalm 12

...with flattering lips and a double heart they speak... those who say, "With our tongue we will prevail, our lips are with us; who is master over us?"

—Psalm 12:2, 4

Have you ever walked through a blinding snowstorm as the wind whistled and snow stung in your eyes? Simply finding your way through seems impossible. This is the image that comes to my mind as I think about the experience of unkind words. Finding refuge from that storm isn't easy.

From this psalm, we see that what makes conversations toxic are lies (Psalm 12:2), boasting (Psalm 12:3), dominating words (Psalm 12:4), and arrogance (Psalm 12:4), to name a few. They come from a place of compulsion. It's as if something is driving our loved one to say these things. As a result, the comments aren't humble or seasoned with grace, and they lack anything that looks for the best in the other person. They startle us. In those moments, the tongue, powerful as it is, seems to prevail.

Yet God is still present and will help us.

The net effect of these words is pain. We don't anticipate conversations going this way and we are surprised by how cruel they are. How does one get over arrows thrown by ones we love? We groan under the weight of such disappointment. Nothing feels right about it, nor do we ever get used to it.

The second effect is prayer. Though the words arise from compulsion, there is something here to be resisted in prayer. God will come to our aid and defend us. He sees our pain and will place us in the safety for which we long.

Difficult as it may seem, it's unwise for us to let those words into our hearts. Even if they are partially true, what do we share with them? We must find our identity in God and the words he speaks. His words are full of grace and hope for a new beginning. Even when he convicts us of something, it is never to crush but to bring something into the light so he can forgive. After that, it is never brought to his memory again. Toxic words are to be quietly resisted, not received.

Dear Father,
Thank you for your pure words. They renew me. Thank you that these toxic words do not determine my future: your words do. Remove from my heart painful words I have let in. Help me discern your words and consistently reject the others. Help me build my life on your faithful words. Have mercy and draw my loved one back into close relationship with you.
In Jesus's name.

WHERE VINDICATION COMES FROM
Day Two
Read Psalm 26

Vindicate me, O Lord, for I have walked in my integrity, and I have trusted in the Lord without wavering.
—Psalm 26:1

I see a picture in my mind. The psalmist has arrows coming at him from multiple directions. The arrows aren't literal; they are lies about him and his character. He didn't look for a fight, nor did he deserve one, but that didn't stop the arrows from coming directly for him. He is confused as to how he could find himself facing this onslaught of ill will. He calls out to God to vindicate him, to declare from heaven, "This man is innocent!"

God is the one who vindicates us, and God alone. We cannot defend ourselves in such conversations and our attempts to do so are generally pointless. The most effective thing we can do amid toxic conversations is usually to practice silence and wait for God to vindicate us. Though he probably won't come through immediately, if we are patient, he will do it. He hears us. He is quite effective when he acts, much more than any attempt on our part at self-defence.

Our confidence comes from being right with God and not being drawn into retaliatory words. Though we aren't perfect, maintaining a calm and trusting disposition throughout a volley of accusation gives us confidence with God, which is better by far than shooting back. It's wise for us to own what we need to own and apologize but not receive accusations into our hearts that are different from what God would say.

Fear and insecurity are often what keep us from maintaining our integrity. The words coming at us seem like the attack of a wild dog with a ferocious bite. In reality, these words are more like a mosquito bite. You feel their sting and afterward they leave a small mark that may itch for a day or two. Your identity, though, is safe with God, who has forgiven you and loves you. Given time, he will vindicate you.

Dear Father,
Thank you for this present difficulty with my loved one, for it causes me to trust in you, and you alone. Forgive me for ways in which I have made the problem worse. Vindicate me. Come to my defence. Help me to be quiet in the face of unfair words and simply trust you. Thank you for hearing my prayer. Give me your peace today.
In Jesus's name, amen.

FINDING FREEDOM FROM TOXIC WORDS

Day Three

Read John 8:31–36

If you abide in my word, you are truly my disciples, and you will know the truth, and the truth will set you free… So if the Son sets you free, you will be free indeed.

—John 8:31–32, 36

It is difficult trying to walk down a pathway with our ankles entangled in rope. Anyone doing that would take the time to shake off the rope, or else they would certainly fall. When we've endured toxic conversations, walking feels like that, only we don't necessarily take the time to shake off the entanglement. Those words affect us, though; they cling to us. Though we didn't deserve it, nor did we provoke it, we can become disentangled.

Jesus tells us that freedom lies in abiding in his word. When we immerse ourselves in his word, we recognize the truth; we are reminded of it and drawn back to it. We see our true identity, for God declares it to us.

However, we can be our own worst enemies if we are prone to fault ourselves when coming out of toxic conversations. Even if we don't blame ourselves, it's not uncommon in such situations for accusations against us to be direct and strong. Our eyes glaze over as these words find their way into our souls. Against that dark backdrop, we need the clarity of the Scriptures to bring us back to how God truly sees us so we can align ourselves with it.

Not only does abiding in the word of God help us with discerning the truth, it also helps us to live differently.

First, we learn to humble ourselves and apologize where we need to own things.

Second, we find grace to serve the very one who is slinging the mud; Christ frees us to do that.

Third, we feel impelled to forgive the one who has spoken so unfairly, and we leave them with Christ.

Fourth, we find courage to set wise boundaries, because we no longer fear our loved ones or look to them for approval.

Fifth, we ask God to heal us. The Scriptures give us hope that he alone breaks ungodly and invisible chains as a result of dark words spoken. He comforts us and heals our tattered emotions. All these come from abiding in his word.

Dear Father,
I know that you see me and the ropes that entangle me. Thank you that I am yours. Set me free from all ungodly entanglement. I forgive my loved one for the hurtful things they have spoken. Forgive me for the grudges I hold onto. Heal my heart. Thank you for setting me free.
In Jesus's name, amen.

DISCERNING THE RIGHT SEASON
Day Four

Read Ecclesiastes 3:1–8

For everything there is a season, and a time for every matter under heaven… [there is] a time to keep silence, and a time to speak…

—Ecclesiastes 3:1, 7

When we find ourselves in difficult seasons of life, it's important to remember that this season won't last forever. There is indeed a time for everything under the sun. There is both a time to keep silence and a time to speak when there are toxic conversations with loved ones going on. Today may not be the best time to help them see how inaccurate their conclusions and beliefs are. It's more challenging to say little in such situations than it is to set them straight. Our fears and anger shout to us to break the silence. Wisdom, though, would usually direct us to stay silent.

I think about some of the plants we own. I'm not an intuitive gardener. Weekly, I fight the urge to water my plants on Wednesday because I so desperately want to see growth. Saturday, however, is watering day. The plants won't thrive if I insist on watering them more than I ought.

With our loved ones, in our zeal to see the growth we long for, the thought of waiting for the correct time for conversations goes against our grain. We would rather simply say things directly and put our thoughts out there. If plants don't respond well to overzealousness, how much more our loved ones? There is a time and season for every matter under heaven.

Not only is there a right time for silence, there's another for speaking. The door for you to speak may open only briefly. You will want to be prepared. Let God also teach you what to say and how to say it. Linger before him in prayer on this.

We are to be led by God. He knows the next move through this unwanted journey and will instruct us. Making that move out of a place of panic is seldom wise. It's better by far to let him teach us when is the right time to speak and when it is best to be silent.

Dear Father,
Thank you that this season I'm in with my loved one will not last forever. Help me recognize what season I'm in and live with wisdom in it. Let me hear your voice so I can maintain silence when words won't help. Help me not to be impulsive but timely in my words, and under your instruction. Don't let my emotions get the best of me. I trust you.
In Jesus's name, amen.

THE VALUE OF BEING SLOW TO ANGER
Day Five
Read Proverbs 15:18

A hot-tempered man stirs up strife, but he who is slow to anger quiets contention.

—Proverbs 15:18

Have you ever burnt yourself badly? One day I burnt my hand when I grabbed the wrong end of a hot curling iron. My hand throbbed with pain for a long time. The only time I felt relief was when I held an ice cube.

That burn reminds me of an angry person and the ice of the one who is patient, as Proverbs teaches us. The one who is slow to anger can calm down an angry individual. Perhaps you, too, have seen the truth of this statement.

Bill sat at a table one Saturday night when we were serving the street-involved people of Toronto. One man was seething angry about something. When Bill asked the man his name, the man screamed at him and began to curse. Bill listened in silence and then waited. As he got up from the table, he quietly said, "I'm glad you're here tonight." That was the end of it. The man was silent. It didn't appear to be the response he had expected.

Addiction seems to breed anger. Not uncommonly, anger in one place tends to breed more anger elsewhere. Careless, insensitive words trigger more of the same. This continues to be the case until someone chooses to overlook a comment and is gracious instead. Until then, toxic conversations and the pain they engender only escalate.

Christ gives us what we need to be slow to anger, even as he is. Choosing a patient and gentle road keeps the relationship intact as you pray and wait for a better day. There is much injustice to be endured in order to be slow to anger, but it's well worth it.

You aren't the only one who must endure these rough waters where it feels like you're being thrown against the rocks. Our prayer for you is that God would give you that disposition that is slow to anger. It is received from heaven, from the one who is rich in patience. He is gracious and consistently slow to anger.

Dear Father,
Thank you for being gracious and patient with me. Help me, in like manner, to be slow to anger. Thank you for the opportunity to learn patience and understanding. I feel my dependence upon you so deeply at this point. Help me not to retaliate but to love as you do. Fill me with your wisdom. Bring us to a new place where words are gentle and healing, helpful at every turn.
In Jesus's name, amen.

UNDERSTANDING SELFISHNESS
Week Nineteen
Introduction

One of the most disturbing moments in one's relationship with a loved one who is addicted is coming face to face with the intense selfishness. I remember it as a child, growing up with a dad who was an alcoholic. He would use our grocery money like it was extra cash to buy liquor and make long-distance phone calls, which at the time were very expensive. One of the biggest reasons my mom kicked my dad out was because we couldn't afford him and his choices.

The thirst for their substance of choice messes with their mind so badly that it seems to completely blind them to what they're saying or doing. The compulsion can be staggering.

Understanding the compulsion is important, though it doesn't make the disillusionment and pain any less on our part. That so much could be overlooked and forgotten in a moment is staggering. Such is the nature of addiction.

None of this is something we get used to. Perhaps it helps to know that it's common among those addicted. When our son became sober, he felt much remorse over choices he had made. With this came many requests for forgiveness. These were beautiful words to hear.

I wish I could say that was the case for my dad and my brother. Sadly, they never did recover from their addiction before passing away.

This week we will consider how best to understand and live with the selfishness that is part of compulsion, and in particular to focus on the help God offers us as we look to him in this challenge. We cannot change the behaviour of our loved one, but neither are we pawns in a game over which we have no control. There is still some good that can be done in each situation.

OVERCOMING OUR OWN SELFISHNESS

Day One

Read Romans 15:1–7

Let each of us please his neighbor for his good, to build him up. For Christ did not please himself...

—Romans 15:2–3

One of the hidden blessings in this unwanted journey is that we are set free from self-absorption. We are stretched to love and pray like we never have. This is seen in several ways.

First, we learn to bear with the failings of our loved one (Romans 15:1). To hold them to our standard is pointless; it only crushes them and serves to create distance in the relationship. They are often aware of their failings, and in many cases loathe themselves as a result. They're unable to meet us on our terms, so we choose, like Christ, to bear with their failings and meet them where they are.

Second, we learn to act for their good, to build them up (Romans 15:2–3). That doesn't mean we ignore our own good or act to our detriment. We cannot ignore our own well-being. We serve them from a position of strength, where we nurture our own souls and care for ourselves. Neither does it mean that we lay down and become a rug to walk on. Rather, we use wisdom so we can build them up in a way that is truly helpful. The point here is that, again like Christ, we don't please ourselves but do those things that are beneficial for our loved one. We act for their sakes. Christ's death on the cross was for our sakes.

Third, we learn to endure (Romans 15:4–5). We generally like immediacy; waiting is not our strong suit. God is known for his great patience. Change doesn't happen immediately. God does so much in the waiting, but our selfish desires can run hard against the call to persevere. Some have already waited a long time to see their loved one find freedom. Remember that we wait for God, not our loved one; we wait for him to fulfill his promises in our loved one.

In this way, we learn to keep the door open to our loved one (Romans 15:7). Very easily, we slam it shut to an ongoing relationship by our tight standards and impatient rigidity. Christ is merciful and teaches us to live selflessly, for the benefit of our loved one, to the glory of God.

Dear Father,
Thank you for being patient with me. Help me to set aside my own demanding and rigid tendencies. Thank you for the encouragement of the Scriptures. Thank you for helping me deal with the challenges that come with waiting. Keep me from erecting barriers out of my impatience. Help me bring down walls with my loved one.
In Jesus's name, amen.

UNDERSTANDING COMPULSION
Day Two
Read James 3:13–18

For where jealousy and selfish ambition exist, there will be disorder and every vile practice. But the wisdom from above is first pure, then peaceable, gentle, open to reason, full of mercy and good fruits, impartial and sincere.
—James 3:16–17

There is always a different way forward than what seems to present itself on this unwanted journey. God fills us with hope even when we see how large the compulsion and resulting self-interest has grown in our relationship with a loved one.

Remember, first, that none of us are devoid of selfishness. Though it's often difficult to recognize in our own lives, we are wise to humble ourselves before God any time we detect self-interest and ask him to change our hearts.

Second, detecting selfishness in our own lives doesn't keep us from looking honestly at the same in our loved one. It just helps us walk humbly. The extent of selfishness in those who are addicted can be staggering. The one who is addicted will at times do anything, say anything, and pay any price to satisfy their desire. This is the nature of compulsion. It manifests as entitlement and self-interest. This one thing is centre in their lives; it controls them. Any relationship is secondary. This is heart-breaking and should drive us to prayer.

Finally, in what feels like the fog of war, remember that the path driven by compulsion is not inevitable. A better way is possible. Hold onto hope. The better way has its source in heaven, not earth. God changes people. If selfish ambition is marked by disorder and evil practices, wisdom from heaven is characterized by purity. This is literally the aroma of heaven. It's always peaceable and gentle. It's not belligerent but open to reason. It's full of mercy and rich with good fruit such that people love to be near it. It's also impartial and sincere.

When compulsion has yielded to heaven's wisdom, sweetness fills both our homes and that person's life. God's ways are always marked by the wisdom of heaven. It is deeply desirable. Pray this. Receive it. Anticipate it.

Dear Father,
Have mercy on me and cleanse me from every selfish way. Help me detect selfish ambition in my own deeds so that I can live with integrity and humility. Keep me from yielding to what seems strong and inevitable where compulsion consumes my loved one at times. Set this one free. Help me to bring the practices of heaven into this relationship daily.
In Jesus's name, amen.

HOW TO KEEP LOVING AMID A CLIMATE OF ENTITLEMENT

Day Three

Read Isaiah 40:27–31

…but they who wait for the Lord shall renew their strength; they shall mount up with wings like eagles; they shall run and not be weary; they shall walk and not faint.

—Isaiah 40:31

The promises of God are our food. They nourish our weary souls and replace destructive thoughts with that which is true and healthy. It reminds me of when we replaced the water line into our house. The line was a hundred years old and made with lead, which can lead to various illnesses.

The backdrop of this verse is weariness, feeling faint, lacking strength, and feeling forgotten by God. It comes from walking this unwanted journey. We are in close proximity with one whose compulsion and resulting self-interest set them at odds with us, which in the end breeds exhaustion. It's like drinking water tainted with lead that poisons us over time. The symptoms are already manifesting themselves.

We need a different water source which comes to us as we wait on the Lord. Those who wait on the Lord are renewed. This person is likened to the eagle which soars to great heights on contrary winds. Though the backdrop is dark and challenging, the one who waits on the Lord is lifted to new heights where they gain a perspective they could never otherwise reach. The one who waits on the Lord is truly lifted up.

Such a person also experiences renewed strength. Weariness loses its grip when we wait on the Lord. The paralyzing power of being overwhelmed is set aside as we suddenly have hope. We don't feel so depleted or discouraged. A strange peace settles upon us. How exactly that exchange happens is difficult to explain. It happens quietly and imperceptibly; it is literally the grace and presence of God.

To wait on the Lord then is to sit quietly with him, to read his word in an unrushed manner, to remember his promises and dwell on them. It is to give thanks to him and enjoy his company. It is to sit with the author of life. As we do that, he gives new thoughts—those that are good and bring health to us.

Dear Father,
I wait upon you. I'm not waiting upon my loved one, but you. You are the source of every good thing. Give me new thoughts as I delight in you. I desire you above all. What does earth have that could satisfy the longing and emptiness of my parched soul? Renew me. Help me to love with a pure heart regardless of what comes before me today.
In Jesus's name, amen.

A PRECIOUS TOOLBOX
Day Four
Read Romans 12:12

Be joyful in hope, patient in affliction, faithful in prayer.

—Romans 12:12, NIV

It is a great day when you receive wise counsel after pouring your heart out over a situation that's tearing you apart. When I read this verse, this is what comes to mind. It's simple, smart, and, by the enabling of the Holy Spirit, doable.

To be joyful in hope is to be overflowing with it. It is to have so much hope that there is a smile on your face. You have hope enough for yourself in your situation as well as others who bump into you. They see your smile; it becomes infectious.

People want to hope and are looking for someone who might lead the way. Who better than those walking through challenging situations? All of this comes from God, who fills us with joyful hope.

To be patient in affliction is to understand that this will pass. It is knowing that God is at work in times of affliction, accomplishing things we don't see, but which given time will become apparent. He is at work in us as he is in our loved one. We are patient because patience welcomes God. It acknowledges him and is an expression of trust in him. Impatience only breeds anger, frustration, and despair; it is altogether unhelpful. Patience is what God produces in us as he works.

Finally, to be faithful in prayer is to never give up praying. To stop praying is to lose hope. Our confidence is in God, and so we call out to him. With him, nothing is impossible. This is where our greatest influence lies.

We will seldom outdistance our prayers. What a privilege it is to be given an audience with the King of Kings, who inquires of us what we would ask of him. What will you ask for? Stay with that request and allow him time. Allow him to change you. He hears your prayer and always does right.

It may seem to be an odd toolbox that the Lord lays at our feet today. It is precious, though, and has in it all that we need. Put it to use. You will be the richer for it.

Dear Father,
Thank you for this toolbox. Fill me with hope until I cannot contain it and it becomes contagious to others around me. Grant me patience in affliction, knowing that you are at work in hardship, changing me as you do my loved one. Grant me a spirit of prayer that calls out to you day and night as I await your intervention in the life of my loved one.
In Jesus's name, amen.

OVERCOMING AMID OPPOSITION
Day Five
Read Psalm 42

...my adversaries taunt me... all the day long, "Where is your God?" Why are you cast down, O my soul, and why are you in turmoil within me? Hope in God; for I shall again praise him, my salvation and my God.

—Psalm 42:10–11

It's challenging to be in a relationship with people in whom compulsion is so strong. What we say and think matters little. Disillusionment often settles into relationships with loved ones who are addicted. Like the psalmist, though, we can learn to overcome.

First, call to God in your pain. The good thing about hardship is that it forces us to seek God earnestly. It takes away mediocrity. Desperation grows, as does one's longing for God. Confidence in God grows as well, though slowly. Like the psalmist, we know God will vindicate us, but it probably won't be quick. It is a good thing that our longing for God grows. It tends to unshackle us from many earthbound concerns that have too strong a grip on us. Who would think that something so unwanted as this journey could become a blessing?

Second, remember that there is more to us than our emotions. The emotions are so alive in this psalm, which is refreshing. Yet they're not our only reality. Though we feel disappointment, abandonment, and loneliness deeply, we can also call them into question. The psalmist even talks to himself. It is better to doubt our emotions than to doubt God. Truth is always deeper.

Third, recall that God has been faithful to you. Remember the things he has done for you. Call them to mind and write them down. Any experience we have in conflict or spiritual darkness must be met with a deeper experience in thanksgiving and praise to God. As Psalm 42:7 says, *"Deep calls to deep..."* The agony of our soul calls to the depth of who God is. The present difficulty is not separated from his past faithfulness. He will come through again, will he not?

Dear Father,
Thank you for inviting my honesty and listening to that which grieves me deeply. Thank you for going deeper than the depth of my deepest emotion, and thank you for meeting me at that place. Thank you for receiving me into your presence every time I come. Pour out your love on me.
In Jesus's name, amen.

THE POWER OF PRAYER AND FASTING
Week Twenty
Introduction

Fasting isn't likely to be anyone's favourite topic. We tend to enjoy eating and make much of it. To be honest, though, there are times in this unwanted journey when we lose all desire to eat. Things become so intense, and perhaps grievous, that we can't even imagine taking anything in. With a broken heart, who wants to eat?

I recall many times when food was distasteful. I simply lost interest. Our loved one didn't want to eat and neither did we. We were so grieved over what has happening in our home. At times like that, fasting was no effort. It became the natural expression of our broken hearts.

Other times, though, fasting is an effective means of prayer by which we are able to express ourselves before God with an urgency we don't usually feel. It also helps us get past superficiality and into the deeper waters where our loved ones swim. We will find ourselves able to attain greater substance in our relationship with God as we fast and seek him more earnestly.

The Scriptures speak of fasting as a valuable discipline. The New Testament doesn't command it, though Jesus assumes that his followers will practice it. It holds great benefit for us in walking this unwanted journey. If you are unfamiliar with fasting, please don't skip over this section of the book. Come open-minded to what may be transformative to you in your journey with your loved one.

We primarily define fasting as a withdrawal from food. This, however, isn't the only type of fast available to us. Some, for health reasons, will not be able to fast from all food. In such cases, one may choose to abstain from sweets, from caffeine, from meat, etc. If none of these are an option, one may choose instead to fast from social media or from spending money.

The point is that great blessings await those who apply this discipline to their lives. Let's explore together the benefits of prayer and fasting.

HOW TO HANDLE DEVASTATING NEWS

Day One

Read Nehemiah 1

As soon as I heard these words I sat down and wept and mourned for days, and I continued fasting and praying before the God of heaven.

—Nehemiah 1:4

How do you handle bad news? In this unwanted journey, there is too much of it. At such times, eating isn't the first thing that comes to mind.

Nehemiah had just received news that Jerusalem, his capital city, had been sacked, its walls destroyed and its people exiled. Upon hearing this, it was as if he lost strength and had to sit down. He became absorbed in the situation as he mourned with fasting and prayer for days on end. He wasn't very good company for his guests, who had come from a distance.

What do you do when your heart simply breaks over what's happening to your loved one? How do you express desperation and urgency? Why not turn to God with fasting?

In that place of long sorrow, a prayer slowly forms. One cannot hasten the process. The confession of sin rises naturally as we are given new insights. We also receive reminders of God's promises. Even hope blossoms as we begin to see how this situation might be turned around.

None of these insights would have been gained by glossing over the pain and disappointment and simply getting on with life.

In addition, Nehemiah came to realize that he had a definite role in achieving a favourable outcome. All of this was borne in a season of fasting.

You too will find that if you put aside food in the midst of your sorrows and present yourself before God in prayer, time will slow down and you'll feel things more deeply, even the disappointments. You'll also hear the voice of God guiding you in how to pray, reminding you of promises and instructing you in the way forward.

There is no shortcut to this. Though in the beginning you may lose interest in food, soon you won't be sure if you want to return to it because of the nearness of God who comforts you in your sorrows. And you know exactly what you need to do.

> Dear Father,
> Thank you for your presence in my sorrows. As I set aside food and present myself before you, instruct my prayers. Take me deeper. Help me to understand this difficulty. Show me my role and instruct me in the way to go. Remind me of your promises. Bring assurance regarding my loved one and comfort me, for my heart is broken.
> In Jesus's name, amen.

FASTING: THE KEY TO GOING DEEPER

Day Two

Read Isaiah 58

Is not this the fast that I choose: to loose the bonds of wickedness, to undo the straps of the yoke, to let the oppressed go free, and to break every yoke?

—Isaiah 58:6

Do you ever wish you could engage more meaningfully in the issues of your loved one? I remember often feeling on the outside of things. How could I go deeper with my loved one? My words seemed shallow and had little effect. He was in a life and death struggle, and I couldn't connect meaningfully. And where was the reality of the power of God?

I never felt that way, though, when I fasted.

As uncomfortable as it is, fasting helps us align with God. We become easily accustomed to patterns in our lives that are unprofitable and pretentious. We're used to going through the motions even in regard to God. As a result, our lives lack power. We look for some magic button, maybe a formula, perhaps recent medical advances to bring release to the bondage of our loved one.

Maybe those pieces can help. However, to overlook that God is calling us back to himself is to miss the most foundational piece. When we fast, we see things in a different light as God puts his finger on what misses the mark. It's in our interest that unprofitable patterns are removed, because they inhibit God's healing and the in-breaking of his light.

Fasting also helps us engage more deeply in the issues of affliction and suffering. Our conversations are often superficial and our experience with suffering limited. We aren't sure that we even want to go there.

Yet we must. But how? When we fast, we're able to identify with our loved one like we never have. Here we find prayers that don't pull back from sorrow but give expression to the urgency of the situation. Fasting gets us past that which is superficial and gets to the reality of human pain. Here we find love like we never knew, love for one in bondage.

Isaiah assures us that all such efforts are rewarded by God with his guiding hand and powerful, life-giving presence.

Dear Father,
Thank you for the promise of engaging deeply with you. Forgive me for patterns I have set that entrench superficiality and keep me from closeness with you as well as my loved one. I don't know how to change that, though I feel desperate for my loved one. As I fast, speak to me and lead me to godly patterns and effective prayers. I am done with that which is trite.
In Jesus's name, amen.

FASTING: HOW TO NAVIGATE AN EVIL DAY
Day Three
Read Matthew 4:1–10

Then Jesus was led up by the Spirit into the wilderness to be tempted by the devil. And after fasting forty days and forty nights, he was hungry.

—Matthew 4:1–2

We find ourselves in a new season, a difficult one unquestionably, yet here we are. The season Jesus found himself in, according to Matthew 4, wasn't one that would be particularly enjoyable. How could it be, being alone in a place of complete abandonment? The wilderness is the haunt of wild animals. It's like a place of the curse. There's nothing there.

It's also a place of troubling darkness. Here, in this place, Jesus encounters the devil. Not uncommonly, the evil one seems near in this season. He discourages and presses us with feelings of hopelessness and depression. He reminds us of our failures and takes advantage of our weaknesses. He waits for moments of greatest weakness and moves in with temptation.

His intention is to move us away from simple trust in God. He intimidates, lies, and casts doubt on the goodness of God, anything so that we might turn from God.

Yet God gave our loved one to us and hasn't abandoned us even in this moment. He also gave us a place of authority in prayer over the evil one in regard to our loved one, ground that ought never to be given up. If we turn away from God, we yield that place to the evil one and all that will follow is confusion. There's so much at risk.

Jesus went into this difficult place with fasting. For forty days, he ate nothing. Though that length of time isn't normative for us, it does point out how to navigate seasons of darkness and loneliness during which we are tempted to lose hope and faith in God.

This is how to find our way through such troubling times when the world seems upside-down and the devil is near. Turn away from food and give yourself to God. You too will be led by him to have answers for the devil in his most terrible temptations and a path forward through this darkness. As Jesus overcame, so too can we.

Dear Father
Thank you that Jesus understands temptation and the darkness of these seasons when the evil one is near. Keep me from doubting your goodness. Help me to constantly lift up prayers for my loved one, knowing that you have given me authority. As I fast and pray, may the victory of Jesus become my portion. Set my loved one free from every chain.
In Jesus's name, amen.

FASTING FOR THE PRESENCE OF GOD
Day Four
Read Matthew 9:14–15

Then the disciples of John came to him, saying, "Why do we and the Pharisees fast, but your disciples do not fast?" And Jesus said to them, "Can the wedding guests mourn as long as the bridegroom is with them? The days will come when the bridegroom is taken away from them, and then they will fast."

—Matthew 9:14–15

If there's anything we need more of in this unwanted journey, it's a greater sense of the presence of God. We know that God is everywhere all the time and that there is nowhere to flee from his presence. However, it is the sense of his presence that we long for. That, more than anything, puts our hearts at rest. We can handle any storm if we know that God is with us.

Jesus connects fasting with his manifest presence. His audience was trying to make sense of why his twelve disciples never fasted. Jesus told them that they would one day understand it—when he was no longer with them. The absence of his presence would trigger their fasting. They would long for him, and that longing would lead them even to set food aside for certain seasons.

Do you long for him? Do you desire a greater sense of his nearness, his comfort, his peace in your struggle? Do you long for his counsel as you're in a difficult place and don't know which way to turn with your loved one? Do you face decisions and lack the courage to make them? Does your heart break over disappointments that leave you despondent and weary? Has your loved one become centre stage to the detriment of all else in your life?

The presence of Jesus fills us with hope and guides us along this difficult pathway. Fasting is key to a greater sense of the presence of Jesus.

Dear Father,
Thank you for giving us the joy of knowing your presence. I love your presence, for you comfort me by it and let me know I am not alone. Many days I long for more of your presence, for the burdens with my loved one are great. Will you not manifest yourself to me in a greater way to show me the way to go? Help me to set aside food to seek you so that your presence would be made manifest to me.
In Jesus's name, amen.

THE REWARD OF FASTING
Day Five
Read Matthew 6:16–18

But when you fast, anoint your head and wash your face, that your fasting may not be seen by others but by your Father who is in secret. And your Father who sees in secret will reward you.

—Matthew 6:17–18

We like to think we aren't motivated by rewards, but it probably isn't true. The reality is that we never outgrow the desire to be rewarded. Though this may not be our main motivation, it factors in and can encourage us to be disciplined in fasting.

Jesus definitely promises a reward for those who fast and pray with true motives. When he mentions a reward, it is to be noted and will be deeply worthwhile.

Jesus again assumes that his followers will fast. He does not command it; it is simply assumed. He knows we will face great difficulties. Looking for a favourable outcome in these desperate scenarios when there is so much to lose, fasting gives expression to our sense of urgency.

Why then the issue of rewards? First, rewards highlight that which is precious to God. He honours what he is looking for. Fasting is an expression of faith in God, and acknowledgment that we are desperate for his intervention and want him more even than food. We are saying that our hope is entirely upon him. He delights in that and rewards it.

Second, rewards point to fasting with pure motives, that which is done quietly and humbly before God as opposed to that which is done to be noticed by people.

Third, rewards can serve to motivate us to stay with it. Fasting is difficult, unquestionably. We easily lose heart because we love to eat. Staying with it, though, is deeply beneficial for these difficult situations with our loved ones.

Fourth, though he does not say what the reward is, it likely manifests both now and in eternity when we'll see him. In the present, God shines his light into the situations for which we seek him. There is always a blessing in the present for those who seek God with fasting. In eternity, he rewards those who have sought him wholeheartedly. Every sacrifice we've made to seek him, including setting aside food, will be rewarded.

Dear Father,
Thank you for rewarding those who diligently seek you. My hope is in you. Perhaps the greatest reward I would seek is to see my loved one set free from every bondage to walk a different path, following you. Reveal yourself. Shine your light. Bring your healing. Show me my role in this. Guide me in how I should pray.
In Jesus's name, amen.

CHOOSING OUR WORDS DETERMINES OUR WAY
Week Twenty-One
Introduction

When our son was in active substance addiction, how we spoke about it mattered. Our words led us to either hope or despair. It wasn't our loved one that brought us to that place; it was our own words. Unquestionably, the challenges that fall to anyone in such a place are large. It's easy to fall into despair and much more challenging to choose hope and stay there.

The battle would begin when he didn't come home when he said he would. We knew he had gone drinking yet again. The knot in my stomach would return. Fear would scream in my head. This would all be followed up by the same well-practiced questions I'd hesitate to say out loud: "Will he make it home safely? Will he lose his wallet this time? Where is he? How long until we know he is back home? How drunk will he be?"

The question we face is how to respond when our loved one has fallen again under the weight of compulsion. Those thoughts are important. Learning a different way to respond is life-giving—for us. It helps us as we try to cope with such a challenging situation.

We recall well the difference that it made as we immediately prayed and found a Bible verse that breathed life into the ditch of our gathered fears.

This week, we will look for new thoughts God offers us to hold onto. We don't have to keep going back to that other way, which is unhelpful to us and won't lead us anywhere good.

WHY HOPEFUL WORDS MATTER
Day One
Read Psalm 19:14

Let the words of my mouth and the meditation of my heart be acceptable in your sight, O Lord, my rock and my redeemer.

—Psalm 19:14

For your own sake, it's important to respond well on those nights when your loved one is off doing something that's destroying them. Our words act like a guide for our heart. Said differently, they act like a floodgate. We choose the flood that will come upon us by our own words. If the words are complaining and hopeless, we soon find ourselves burdened with a despondent spirit. If the words are guarded and express trust in God, we actually feel hope. Our words have considerable influence over our own souls.

Some difficulties arise, though. One is that our default response is often quite strong. That first reaction, probably negative, directs the flood that follows. Can we arrest those first words which come out of our mouths? It's not too late to shut one floodgate and open another that's more hopeful.

A second challenge is managing to say something other than the obvious. If our loved one has fallen again, we can't think of anything hopeful to say. We have perhaps learnt to simply say things the way they are.

However, does all truth need to be spoken? Some of our words bring oppressive suitcases with them. At first mention, we begin unpacking them in our own souls. Those complaining words we felt so entitled to are soon shown to be entirely unprofitable because of the power they exert over us. Had we chosen instead to make the words of our mouth acceptable in God's sight, we would find ourselves in a much more hopeful place. We are being tricked by the father of lies in our conviction to say things that spring from what seems obvious.

There is always a deeper truth than what meets the eye. God is at work, listening to our prayers. To hold to a complaining view of our loved one is to bring ourselves to a hopeless place. Thus we need to make our words guarded and our conversation more prayerful. This acknowledges God and shuts the door to impending darkness.

Dear Father,
Thank you for your righteous rule in all things. I acknowledge your presence with me and your faithfulness. May all my words and thoughts be pleasing to you. Forgive me for allowing my words to run away on me and become faithless. I choose to trust you and acknowledge you regardless of what comes to me today.
In Jesus's name, amen.

WHEN THANKFULNESS IS A HARD CHOICE
Day Two
Read Habakkuk 3:17–19

Though the fig tree should not blossom, nor fruit be on the vines, the produce of the olive fail and the fields yield no food, the flock be cut off from the fold and there be no herd in the stalls, yet I will rejoice in the Lord; I will take joy in the God of my salvation. God, the Lord, is my strength; he makes my feet like the deer's; he makes me tread on my high places.

—Habakkuk 3:17–19

It is a dark day when our eyes are stuck on that which is sad and gloomy. It comes easily to us, perhaps. What's unnatural is choosing to put our hope in God when nothing looks like it is going our way.

The prophet Habakkuk describes a scene where the crops have failed completely. In addition, the barn has no livestock in it. Perhaps the animals died as a result of the crop failure. In any case, in an agrarian society, this is as bad as it gets. The future is as dismal as the present.

The choice we can make at this point is to yet rejoice in God. Though it seems counterintuitive, our words will bring us to a different place. Regardless of what's happening before our eyes, it is possible to still rejoice in God—not for all the dead crops or the empty stalls, but rather because God is still our Saviour, our strength. Do we find hope and strength only from what our eyes see? Has God suddenly ceased to be worthy of praise because of our hardships?

As we give thanks to God in the midst of difficulty, we find that our steps become lighter. We are suddenly able to climb to the heights. This is an upward climb through difficulty to a place we have never been, a place we never even thought possible. The mountain that stood before us is now under our feet. What changed is that we chose to rejoice in God, though the entire picture looked bleak.

The surprise for us is that the view from the top is spectacular. It's a view we have never taken in before. And it only comes to those who learn to rejoice in God in the middle of hardship.

Dear Father,
Unshackle my eyes from what is visible. Give me eyes to see you and perceive the greatness of your kingdom. Thank you for your unchanging love for me and my loved one. I choose to give thanks and acknowledge you amid our present difficulties. I take joy in you. Only you can make me climb these heights. Thank you for your grace.
In Jesus's name, amen.

BENEFITS TO LETTING YOUR WORDS LEAD YOU TO A DIFFERENT PLACE

Day Three

Read 1 Peter 3:8–12

Do not repay evil for evil or reviling for reviling, but on the contrary, bless, for to this you were called, that you may obtain a blessing… "For the eyes of the Lord are on the righteous, and his ears are open to their prayer. But the face of the Lord is against those who do evil."

—1 Peter 3:9, 12

There are two kinds of people described in this passage. The first are those who repay evil for evil. Unkind words spoken breed the same. This kind of relationship is common and comes naturally to us.

The second is different. When we are reviled, we bless. Though harsh words land upon us, we choose instead to speak kindly and with grace. This kind of response leads us to a new and desirable place in several ways, though it's contrary to human nature.

First, it is our vocation, given us by God. If we are called to it, that is the place where we will feel alive and experience the nearness of God. What he calls us to, difficult though it may be, is what we were made for.

Second, here we experience the blessing of God—and that is desirable! The pathway to receive blessing from God is to bless another, even if our loved one has said some very unkind words to us. This is a place of fruitfulness and effectiveness. To be without God's blessing is to live an empty life. We are wise to pursue God's blessing.

Third, words of blessing keep us in the place where our prayers are answered. Dipping into retaliation threatens our effective prayer. Often, when it comes to our loved ones, all we have is prayer. There is so much that cannot be said. The channels of prayer must be kept open or else we'll be left to our own resources. We need God to hear our pleas for mercy, protection, wisdom, and strength. Let us hold back our harsh words and speak graciously, lest we lose the place of confidence in prayer.

Finally, we risk the friendship of God when we return insult for insult. We need God's favour in order for us to live as we ought. Our own words, chosen wisely, lead us to that place and keep us there.

Dear Father,
Thank you for helping me to bless those who curse me. Forgive me for when I have fallen into returning insult for insult. Set me free from retaliatory urges. Lead me in the path of peace. I trust you to vindicate and defend me. Thank you for your favour. I choose your way and turn away from what seems natural to me.
In Jesus's name, amen.

THERE'S SO MUCH AT RISK

Day Four

Read Ephesians 4:29–32

Let no corrupting talk come out of your mouths, but only such as is good for building up… that it may give grace to those who hear. And do not grieve the Holy Spirit of God, by whom you were sealed for the day of redemption… Be kind to one another, tenderhearted, forgiving one another, as God in Christ forgave you.

—Ephesians 4:29–31, 32

We lose so much when we say things we regret. First, the impact on our loved one can be devastating. If they're looking for reasons to fault us, at such moments we definitely give them what they seek. Honourable speech robs them of that opportunity and keeps them simply having to deal with themselves, which is where the focus should be.

In addition, if they fly off the handle regularly, we may think it wouldn't be a big deal for us to lash out at them. Good leadership, though, especially in conflict, comes from being grounded in the hope that God gives. If we lose hope, we begin to speak words that lack grace.

Even as we feel in conflict with our loved one, they still look to us for stability. Our words are to give grace to those who hear, even if their words aren't gracious. When our words no longer serve the purpose of building them up, they are no longer helpful. It's like having a rainstorm fall on land that's already flooded.

Second, losing control impacts our relationship with God. When we resort to the manner of words we receive from our loved one, these are not words worthy of the Holy Spirit who lives in us. We risk grieving him. If we grieve him, we have lost our effectiveness and impact. We need everything God is willing to give us on this unwanted journey. He is our only hope. How could we grieve him at such a time?

Third, we sell ourselves short. We were meant for more than this. Our words can be better. As Christ forgave, so should we. He accepts us and shows it by his kindness and mercy. We can do likewise by his strength.

As much as we feel it is a day for justice to be done, we are wiser to let mercy have the upper hand and leave justice with God. Let our words lead us to a better place.

Dear Father,
Thank you for having been merciful to me. Help me to lead my loved one with words that are like yours, not theirs. Fill me with hope. Give me self-restraint that does not grieve you. I need you more than anything. Thank you for your mercy.
In Jesus's name, amen.

THE IMPACT OF SCRIPTURE ON OUR WORDS
Day Five
Read Psalm 119:105

Your word is a lamp to my feet and a light to my path.

—Psalm 119:105

Our words determine where our feet will travel, with our mind and heart in tow. It's a popular notion to think and speak positive thoughts. There is some truth in this. People recognize the significance of our own words on us.

The psalmist goes further, though. Our words can lead us into sunshine or a stormy day, but where will our words take their cue from? The Word of God lights our pathway. The words we listen to in the Scriptures inform the direction for our feet, just as they do the words we speak.

The Scriptures are light for our darkness because they change the way we speak. If we want to speak different words, we are wise to get into the Scriptures and live there. The word of God renews our mind so that our old patterns of thought lose their grip on us, as do old patterns of speaking. We will find ourselves becoming more hopeful, which in turn will change the words that come from our mouths. We are changed by the word of God.

The Scriptures are also light in our darkness because they make plain the path that is difficult to see. The Scriptures light the way before us. Some paths are well-lit and we wouldn't think to take a light. Some paths, however, are barely discernible.

When we walk with an addict or someone struggling with mental illness, it can truly feel like the middle of a vast forest where there is little light and the way through seems hidden. God's word plays an important role in every aspect of our lives. Every day it lights the pathway for us that was not visible. Without that light, we wouldn't know which way to go.

Our hearts and minds will follow the lead of God's word. This will only happen if we read it. Take time daily in the Scriptures. Let them guide you, comfort you, and lead you into a place of peace amid the storm.

Dear Father,
Thank you for your word, which helps me find a new song to sing when all seems grey and hopeless. Renew my mind through your word so I can speak in a way that honours you. Light the path for me that seems hidden. Show me the way. Give me the wisdom I need today. Fill me with courage. Strengthen me and point me in the right direction. Thank you, Father.
In Jesus's name, amen.

WHO TAKES CENTRE STAGE, GOD OR YOUR LOVED ONE?
Week Twenty-Two
Introduction

It's quite common for whatever occupies my mind to become all-consuming if I'm not careful. If you have a sick child, parent, or friend, you will understand. The one who needs you most gets your attention and energy.

Where is the balance in all this? Is there an alternative?

I remember a particular day when our son had gone out drinking. The anxiety I struggled with was often overwhelming. I called Bill to let him know. On this day, he shared something with me that stopped me in my tracks. He said that as he had been praying for our son that morning, the Lord had spoken to him, saying, "How is it that your son has taken centre stage in your life?"

These things happen subtly and without effort. Every conversation can become about this one who is struggling. Fears over what will happen with them can dominate all else. A certain dread may arise. Soon this loved one has taken a central place in your life and is the focus of your mental energy. God is off to the side somewhere.

As a result, exhaustion and discouragement are never far behind. When God is no longer the rock upon which we stand, we find ourselves like ships without a rudder. We stand on shifting sand.

This week we will look at Scriptures which point us back to God and the centre place he alone deserves in our lives.

THE VALUE OF SITTING WITH JESUS

Day One
Read Luke 10:38–42

But the Lord answered her, "Martha, Martha, you are anxious and troubled about many things, but one thing is necessary. Mary has chosen the good portion, which will not be taken away from her."

—Luke 10:41–42

Martha is a thoughtful woman. She opened her home to Jesus, after all! Martha, however, was also a practical woman who had plans that included her sister. Someone important had come to their home and there was a need to be hospitable and of course put on a nice spread. In her mind, what needed to be done was of greater importance than sitting with Jesus.

Martha's whole goal was to care for the needs of those in her home, but she was misguided. It led her to be agitated and frustrated, all the more as her sister sat at the feet of Jesus.

Those who have someone struggling to move forward in life because of addiction struggle with the same thing. Jesus wasn't saying that what Martha did wasn't important, but that what Mary did was better. It is hard to sit like Mary when we see so clearly what logically needs to get done!

By his presence, Jesus gives us life. Sitting with him is more precious and transformative than any task we could busy ourselves with. Time spent with Jesus changes us; it gives us new insights and sets us free from anxiety. His words are life. Once we've tasted the goodness of God, we long for those moments when we can be still with him.

Many good things can be done to help your loved one in this moment. None, however, is more important than taking some time to sit quietly with Jesus. It's important to work from a place of rest and a full cup.

It seems to me that if there was one thing Jesus would want to say to you today, it is this: "Sit with me first. Be still and know that I am God. I know what needs doing today. Rest in me. Let me strengthen you and bring you peace."

Dear Father,
How often the urgent drags me away from what is important. Forgive me for the times when I fail to sit with you and wait to hear what it is you want to say to me. I choose to quiet myself in your presence and wait for you today. Speak to me and teach me what I need to learn.
In Jesus's name, amen.

HOW TO STAY CENTRED ON GOD

Day Two

Read Mark 12:28–34

And you shall love the Lord your God with all your heart and with all your soul and with all your mind and with all your strength.

—Mark 12:30

I was about twelve years old when I started to play baseball. One day, I was distracted when the ball was thrown to me and it hit me just above my eye. My injury resulted in a black eye. When your head isn't in the game, things can go badly.

Jesus said that what truly matters to God is being fully devoted to him with all that we are. He wants our full attention. When we lose sight of him amid the heartbreak and sorrow, we lose our grounding and find ourselves preoccupied with lesser things. Keeping Christ centre stage anchors us amid the tsunami of trials and keeps us gazing at the only one who can give us life.

How does one remain centred on God amid the intense disappointments and sorrow that accompany loving someone who is addicted? Faith in God isn't only for sunny days when all is going our way. It's all the more for when we find ourselves in storms and in a sea of indifference.

What truly matters, said Jesus, is to be fully given to him, even at such a time as this. To keep him centre stage, especially now, is the key to navigating such turbulent times, waiting quietly upon him, praying to him. In him lies the wisdom and strength that are essential for the challenges of this day. Allowing our minds to become distracted by the disappointments of life can cause us to lose quiet focus on God and fall into a dark and hopeless place. Give thanks and listen to him. Make room for God to fill your thoughts.

We give too much power to whatever it is that throws our affections off God. This is the perfect time to open the word of God and linger quietly there as you read. God will help you come back to the place where he is the centre and all else moves to the periphery.

Dear Father,
Thank you for your love for me. Forgive me for drifting from wholehearted love for you. Heal me of my fears and insecurities that I might not be thrown off so easily by what comes at me. Speak to me so that I might find comfort and direction amid the disappointments. Only you have words of life. I rest in you and wait for you.
In Jesus's name, amen.

DON'T WAIT FOR THINGS TO IMPROVE

Day Three

Read Matthew 6:25–34

But seek first the kingdom of God and his righteousness, and all these things will be added to you.

—Matthew 6:33

Waiting in quiet trust for the goodness of God, even in the rough spots, is lifegiving. It sounds like a perfect focus for when you're on vacation, but what about now when anxiety threatens over the state of your loved one?

Jesus pointed out that our anxiety isn't only futile, it's unprofitable. We change nothing by it. Though Jesus was speaking to people who felt insecure over provision of food, drink, and clothing, the same applies to our desire to have things settled with regard to our loved one. How can we keep God centre when our loved one's life is going off the rails? Does that situation not preoccupy us completely?

The point here is that our Father in heaven is familiar with all our burdens. We cry out to him with a broken heart. Of course he knows. Can we rest in his goodness even with all the loose ends?

Have you tasted his goodness before? He hasn't changed, though you presently walk a dark path. Once we have tasted his goodness, we won't want anything else. His goodness is experienced as peace.

He also demonstrates it by the way he cares for us and watches over our loved one. He will watch over you and give you all that you need. He will comfort you and manifest his wisdom to you. He will perform miracles along the way and satisfy you with his love.

Childlike trust is where it's at. We are taught to simply trust in God, even while we are in a place of great need and cannot predict the outcome. Jesus says there is a reward for people who seek him first. We can trust him to overcome the things we previously obsessed about. His promise that all this will be added to us is of great worth to us and certainly cannot be purchased anywhere.

Dear Father,
I yield myself quietly to you, like a child. Forgive me for losing sight of your goodness. Help me live with mystery and not try to figure everything out. I know you can be trusted. Today I seek your will and your ways. I rest in you. I present my loved one before you in the name of Jesus. O God, deliver this one. And satisfy me today with your love.
In Jesus's name, amen.

WAYS THAT GOD HELPS US STAY CENTRED ON HIM
Day Four
Read Matthew 14:22–33

And when they got into the boat, the wind ceased. And those in the boat worshiped him, saying, "Truly you are the Son of God."

—Matthew 14:32–33

On this unwanted journey, God does many things to help us keep our focus on him. First, he meets us in our exhaustion.

The story from today's passage unfolds somewhere between 3:00 and 6:00 a.m. The disciples have been at the oars for many hours, having made little headway. The chances are high that they were exhausted.

Where exhaustion and despair settle in upon us, Christ comes out and meets us where we are.

Second, when we feel utterly alone and beyond help, Christ finds a way into that impossible place. Nobody had ever heard of someone walking on the water. Understandably, the disciples thought Jesus to be a ghost. God will manifest himself to you in ways and at times that will surprise you. He sends people, gives gifts, performs miracles, etc. To encourage you and keep your eyes centred on him, there is no dark place he will not walk into.

Third, he will cause you to rise above the very storm that was making the way so hard for you.

Peter, seeing Jesus walk on the water, boldly asked if he could do the same. Jesus invited him to, and amazingly Peter did actually walk on the tumultuous sea.

There may be moments when you have experienced this. The wind rages but you are well because your eyes are fixed on Jesus. God wants to increase those moments until we experience his presence each day.

Fourth, when we lose sight of him and the storm again takes our focus, Jesus quickly reaches out and rescues us. Anytime he is not our centre in the storm, the outcome is the same: fear overtakes us. However, in his mercy, he saves us when we cry out to him.

Finally, he gets into our boat and calms the storm. He doesn't always calm it. But if he is in the boat, that's what matters. The text says that the disciples worshipped him when they saw this. Jesus is where he should be again: centre stage.

Dear Father,
Thank you for your grace. I have much weakness, but you come to me and help to keep you centre. Your provision and kindness help me to walk this journey. I praise you for your great mercy to me. Help me today to keep you in the centre of my gaze.
In Jesus's name, amen.

KEEPING OUR HOPE FIXED ON GOD ALONE

Day Five

Read Colossians 2:9–10

For in him the whole fullness of deity dwells bodily, and you have been filled in him, who is the head of all rule and authority.

—Colossians 2:9–10

It was a Monday morning when I visited the doctor's office with our son. He was extremely depressed and wanted his life to come to an end. He had been in his first rehab just two days prior but had begged us to let him leave. The decision really was not ours to make, so reluctantly we had agreed.

I watched him walk into the doctor's office that day, my heart broken. Hopelessness flooded my mind. Then, ever so quietly, I heard that still, small voice: *"Do not put your hope in your son. Put it in me."*

Today's Scripture reminds us of the one in whom we put all our hope. Christ lacks nothing. He knows no limitation. He is complete in power, love, knowledge, and wisdom. Every perfection is embodied in him.

He also possesses all authority. There is no name greater than his. What he decides will be accomplished. He always was and always will be. In this present moment, he sustains everything by his word. To set our hope upon him is to place our hope well. To pray to him about our loved ones is the very best thing we can do.

I know nothing about cars. I know how to fill them with gas and how to drive them. That's basically where it ends. Bill definitely knows more, but even his understanding is limited. If you have a problem with your car, you would be taking a risk to ask us what's wrong with it. You would be better off taking it to a shop that can do proper diagnostics and pin down the problem and actually fix it.

As humans, we are just as limited when it comes to the heart. We think we know what must be done. Perhaps we're right. However, we would be wiser to go to the one who definitely knows and has the power and authority to do what is needed. God is up for the task, and for this we are all so thankful!

Dear Father,
Thank you for having given us one who is above all and for placing us in him. You have filled us and given us all we need. I wait upon you today with thanksgiving and quiet trust. You give me rest. Would you care for my loved one? Would you direct their steps today? Give them wisdom beyond themselves and watch over their life.
In Jesus's name, amen.

THE FOLLY OF PRESUMPTION
Week Twenty-Three
Introduction

Early one morning, Bill sat alone in silence and prayer. It had been a difficult night. Our son had been out drinking but had found his way home. He would be sleeping in, as would the rest of the household, each one of us relieved though sad and exhausted.

Bill felt discouraged and was grasping at hope. He wondered, almost out loud, "Where do I find encouragement? Is there any encouragement? How is this even the same boy we once knew?"

As he mused in those early morning hours, certain larger questions began to form.

"What will happen to our boy? Where will this road lead?"

All we could see was growing disorder and a life increasingly out of control. Our son's innocence was gone altogether. The more Bill thought on it, the darker and more depressing the situation seemed. Hope was fading quickly.

Then Bill noticed our son's shoes. Our son had always taken good care of his shoes, ever since he was young. Though he had stumbled home so drunk tonight, barely able to navigate our stairs, feeling both sick and tormented, there were his shoes, perfectly placed beside each other. It was exactly as he had always done.

Even in his drunkenness, he had managed to meticulously care for his shoes. How he managed to do this was beyond us. It was as if God were saying to Bill, *"He is still the same boy, none other. The darkness is not as deep as you make it out to be. He has not abandoned all the good he once knew."*

All at once, Bill was filled with gratitude and hope. All this from a pair of shoes.

It's easy for us to despair and presume upon the future with our many fears, predicting where this unwanted journey will go. We are not given that. We are unwise to make such predictions in our hearts. We unwittingly rob ourselves of hope by saying things we really have no clue about.

God's reach and power is greater than the deepest brokenness of our loved ones. Is it all really as bad as we make it out to be? When we reach out to God in our desperation, will he not bring light to our hearts? He will encourage us with hope and help us to see from a different perspective. He will help us see what he sees. He will give us hope—and hope is what we need if we are to survive this journey.

This week we want to discuss our tendency towards presumption with a view to strengthening our hearts with hope.

FIGHTING AGAINST BAD NEWS

Day One
Read Psalm 27:13

I believe that I shall look upon the goodness of the Lord in the land of the living!

—Psalm 27:13

One day my mother phoned Bill and me to let us know that my brother had been taken by ambulance to the hospital. When we got there, he was in the ICU. He had such a cocktail of self-medicated drugs in him that he'd gone into cardiac arrest. My poor mom had thought he was unresponsive from having taken a long nap, and when she'd finally tried to awaken him it had become clear that this was something much different.

When we sat with the attending doctor, the prognosis was awful. He clearly didn't think my brother would live and said as much. Bill and I began to pray in earnest for him.

The next day when we visited again, a couple of nurses approached us. One of them said, "You must be Christians."

We asked them why they would say that.

"No one comes back from blood pressure numbers that low," the other said. "You must have been praying."

Today's verse, one which I have often copied out and hung where I can see it, came racing to mind: *"I believe that I shall look upon the goodness of the Lord in the land of the living!"*

God is still in charge, even in dark places. The darkness may seem overwhelming to us, but it's not beyond his reach. He holds authority in those hopeless realms. As we pray, he hears us and acts. Prayer in that place of darkness only comes from people who believe that the goodness of God will be seen in the situation. If we're overtaken by hopelessness, we won't pray with any confidence. We can trust God to manifest his goodness somehow in the darkest situations.

God asks us to wait on him even in the middle of bad news. As long as our loved ones are in the land of the living, we are encouraged to take confidence in this: that we will see the goodness of God. And we are to pray accordingly.

Dear Father,
Thank you for sitting with me in dark places. Even when evil seems to have won the day, I will wait on you, for your authority reaches deeper and your love goes further. I will seek you and pray because your goodness is not cancelled by bad news. Save my loved one. Protect this one from all evil. Visit us with your healing. Give me courage for the next step.
In Jesus's name, amen.

HOW TO FIND HOPE WHEN NOBODY ELSE DOES

Day Two
Read Acts 27

When neither sun nor stars appeared for many days, and no small tempest lay on us, all hope of our being saved was at last abandoned.

—Acts 27:20

Complete hopelessness had gripped everyone on board that ship, all 276 persons—all but Paul and his friends. Their ship had been caught in a cyclone and they were being driven helplessly in an unwanted direction. Their entire effort now went towards survival. To make matters worse, they couldn't get their bearings as the sun and stars were blotted out. They were so frightened that no one ate. They truly thought this was their end.

Again, except Paul and his friends.

How does one avoid being drawn into despair when the evidence is so strong to the contrary? First, ask God for a word to give you hope. God came to Paul in the night and told him personally that he must reach his destination and why. God still does that. He will reveal himself to those who seek him in storms and somehow give a message to help.

Next, keep praying for your loved one. God said to Paul that everyone with him would live. They were safe because Paul was asking for their lives to be spared. Earlier in the story, he had told the captain that their voyage would be met with loss of ship and lives. He was asking God to save them all.

Are you convinced that God hears your urgent prayers regarding your loved one and that prayer actually changes things?

Lastly, don't doubt what God says to you. It's as if, with sun and stars no longer in view, the only light remaining is the one God shone through his listening servant. Everyone looked to Paul. Though at the beginning of the story he was just another prisoner, at the end he basically commanded the ship.

If you're getting your bearings from any source other than the living God, you will lose hope, as will those around you. God is the source of hope, and he doesn't work according to the thinking of the majority.

Dear Father,
Thank you for the light you have shone in my heart. I quiet myself in the storm and wait for you. Give me a word to strengthen me and provide direction to this situation that seems beyond control. Thank you for intervening in all things for those who seek you. Have mercy on my loved one.
In Jesus's name, amen.

THE PRESUMPTION OF STORMS

Day Three

Read Isaiah 26:3

You keep him in perfect peace whose mind is stayed on you, because he trusts in you.

—Isaiah 26:3

There is a famous picture of a bird perched on top of a rock while the waves surge all around it. The bird is unmoved. One would think the small creature should be frightened and fly away to some more idyllic setting, since the storm carries tremendous power and threatens that little life. The bird, however, is steadfast, content even though everything around it is a churning fury. The rock it rests on isn't going anywhere.

Storms are presumptuous. They scream too loudly. They always do. Storms threaten and intimidate. They throw a mighty punch, but they're too loud. They give the impression of being all-powerful. They threaten utter destruction. They exalt themselves as if none can hide from their terror. However, this is not the case.

God alone is all-powerful. He is a mighty rock and those who stand on him are unmoved regardless of how terrible the storm is. Storms never move God, nor do they frighten him. In like manner, he gives perfect peace to the one whose mind is stayed on him. That would be frustrating to the storm that boasts omnipotence.

The person who has come to know that God is a mighty rock under her feet will also recognize the presumption of storms. We cannot attribute to storms qualities that only belong to God. They do not deserve the fear and terror we give them. Immovability belongs to the one who is rooted and grounded in Christ.

It's not really that challenging to have peace on a quiet and calm day. Experiencing it when the winds howl is a function of one who has come to recognize the greatness of God and the presumption of storms. Though we get worn down by them, God keeps us in his tender care and grants us a firm place to stand. He will watch over your life.

Dear Father,

Thank you for promising peace as we keep our minds locked on you. Forgive me for attributing to the storm that which only belongs to you. I place my confidence in you to help and heal. Deliver me from my fears. Thank you for rooting and grounding me in Christ. Help me rest in you and reach out to you in the storm. Watch over my loved one. Keep this one safe in the palm of your great hand.

In Jesus's name, amen.

THE PRESUMPTION OF PREDICTING OUTCOME
Day Four

Read Jeremiah 29:11–14

For I know the plans I have for you, declares the Lord, plans for welfare and not for evil, to give you a future and a hope. Then you will call upon me and come and pray to me, and I will hear you. You will seek me and find me, when you seek me with all your heart. I will be found by you…

—Jeremiah 29:11–14

In this passage, the prophet addresses people who are going into political exile for seventy years; he tells them in advance. Yet even as he declares this, he brings a tender promise from God that goes even further down the road. He says that God alone holds the future and that after a season of difficulty he will rescue them, bringing them back to their homeland, creating deeply desirable days to come.

God's promise to us, even at the beginning of this unwanted journey, is for a good future filled with hope. Never lose that.

Yet this does not exempt us from suffering, nor does it guarantee a certain outcome. We have attended too many funerals of addicted and struggling people to say that.

The threat against our loved one is real, though death is not inevitable. It is presumptuous to say that this journey will end in disaster. It's not given to us to say that, even under our breath, or even to think it. Rather, we are urged to go to God in prayer and plead for a different outcome. Let him say what the future holds in answer to our prayers. Actively wait on him. He alone has power to see the future and declare it, unlike us. Remember too that our prayers do affect the outcome. Will he not speak to your heart and fill you with hope?

God knows the beginning from the end and promises to be with us. We are bound to him and he to us, through Christ. He alone knows the way through this wilderness; what is given to us is to humbly follow. There is no other way to walk this journey than to stick close to him.

The future is not dark, as it seems, when God is in the picture.

Dear Father,
Thank you for your faithful promise to me. Thank you that, though you hold the future, our prayers do affect the outcome. Though there is much I don't understand, I know that you hear me. Have mercy on my loved one. Reveal yourself to this one so precious to me and save their life. Thank you for a desirable future and a strong hope.
In Jesus's name, amen.

HOW TO THINK ABOUT THINGS FUTURE

Day Five

Read Daniel 3

If this be so, our God whom we serve is able to deliver us from the burning fiery furnace, and he will deliver us out of your hand, O king. But if not, be it known to you, O king, that we will not serve your gods or worship the golden image that you have set up.

—Daniel 3:17–18

Any attempt at projecting the future must be held loosely. In this case, the Jews were exiles in a foreign land whose king was arrogant. He erected a great golden statue of himself and required all his subjects to bow before it in worship.

Shadrach, Meshach, and Abednego may have been far from home, but they would not compromise their standards; they refused to worship anyone but God. That decision threw them into immediate conflict with the king.

It also helps us navigate how to think about things future.

First, never let go of your faith in God. Even if nobody is watching, it's not worth it to compromise your standards. Be true to God. To have his favour is more precious than any advantage that earth offers, even if it costs you.

Second, trust in God to deliver you and come to your aid. Even if you're the only one in a large crowd doing so, hope in God. Everyone watching may presume how this story will end; most certainly, these three men will be incinerated. The three, however, are unmoved in their conviction. They believe God will come to their aid.

Are you confident in the goodness of God, that he hears your prayer and will come to your aid?

Lastly, hold outcomes loosely. There is the possibility that things will turn out different than what we expect. Like them, we don't really know! We simply believe that God is faithful to those who are faithful to him. We choose to follow God regardless of the future.

Though we cannot predict the outcome of our days, we are not robbed of confidence in prayer. God is not a vending machine, but he is always good. In the end, God marvellously delivered the three. The best way to walk confidently with the future in sight is with faith in God.

Dear Father,
Thank you for coming to the aid of those who trust you. May my faith mature so that I look to you, not the masses. Help me walk this lonely road with my eyes fixed on you alone. Thank you for the example of these three men. I will trust your goodness and pray in faith, leaving the outcome with you. I know you are always good.
In Jesus's name, amen.

A HOLY PARTNERSHIP
Week Twenty-Four
Introduction

There is no end of things we would love to do for our loved ones, so many ways in which we think we could make the way forward easier for them. This sometimes causes us to intervene in ways that are unprofitable. We plan all sorts of great things, but God can outdo us any day of the week. He alone has the power to tinker in the hearts of people. We do not. We think if we just do this or that, they'll stop doing what they're doing. If only it were that easy.

We must come to the place of realizing that all our helping, though borne out of hearts of love, can become a stumbling block to our loved ones' recovery or maturity. Resting and choosing not to react to every episode of drama, whatever the source, is a step in the right direction.

This doesn't mean we will do nothing, nor that God encourages us to be passive. To the contrary, he calls us into a holy partnership and leads us to definitely do things. Those acts should be taken under his instruction, though, and not in attempts at rescuing our loved one. We are wise to trust God to do what only he can do rather than exhaust ourselves doing things he does not mean for us to do.

This week we will focus on this truth: we should let God do what only he can do and do instead those things he calls us to do.

TRUSTING THE POTTER WITH THE CLAY

Day One

Read Jeremiah 18:1–6

O house of Israel, can I not do with you as this potter has done? declares the Lord. Behold, like the clay in the potter's hand, so are you in my hand, O house of Israel.

—Jeremiah 18:6

It's important to remember that we are not God. He is the potter and we are the clay. He makes and moulds us according to his plans. This also includes our loved ones. While it may be true that compulsion is getting the better of our loved ones, they are yet on his wheel and in his sight.

The prophet was writing about people who did not yield to God and yet were on his pottery wheel. He holds authority over our lives whether or not we submit to him.

When a potter is about to do an intricate work upon his clay piece, he slows down, leans in, and adds the details carefully. The eye cannot wander from the work that is before him, even for a moment. God's eye is fixed on us as it is on our loved one. He is fashioning something beautiful in us even through our difficulties.

Do not think that he has taken his eye off you just because of the turbulence you are experiencing. Truly, we are being changed through hardship, becoming more trusting of God, more prayerful, and more thankful. This is because the potter has his eye fixed upon us and is skillful in what he does. He has not abandoned us.

It is good to remember that we are not the potter in our loved ones' lives either. God doesn't invite us to sit at the wheel. He alone moulds and crafts according to his wisdom. It's easy for us to step in and take the role of the potter in their lives, but we don't possess that ability.

We do have a role, but it is to live under his instruction as he moulds the life of our loved one. He sees what we cannot and knows what is needed. We should ask him how we should pray and what he would have us do… but we must let him be the potter.

Dear Father,
You are the potter and I am the clay. Thank you for all that you have done in me through this unwanted journey. Thank you that your eye is upon me, as it is on my loved one. Forgive me for thinking that I am the potter in the life of my loved one. I trust you. I want to walk under your instruction. Teach me how to pray for this one.
In Jesus's name, amen.

GAINING WISDOM FROM GOD
Day Two
Read Job 38

Who is this that darkens counsel by words without knowledge?

—Job 38:2

When times of hardship come, we struggle to make sense of things and sometimes question God in the process. He is certainly up for our many questions and can handle our lament, which speaks carelessly at times out of pain.

The story of Job is helpful for us. It is the story of a wealthy man with a large family who suffered tremendous loss, even of his children and health. In the end, God mercifully vindicated and blessed him.

From this we learn some valuable lessons. We are reminded that we are not God. Like Job, we grasp at answers and struggle to understand. The truth is that we are deeply limited in our comprehension of our own difficulties. God alone has perfect knowledge and sees through all things. Unless we ask him for wisdom in regard to the complex issues of our loved ones, our perception will almost certainly be skewed.

Also, it is unwise for us to turn against him just because we don't understand or approve of this unwanted journey. Many do. Job's wife advised him to curse God. Hardship hits our sense of entitlement. We deserve better than this, we think. Do we not see, however, that hardship is a much better teacher than ease? Do we accept only good from God's hand and not trouble? Do we have to understand everything to trust him? Surely there is great mystery in following him. He is God, after all, trustworthy and good in all his ways.

Finally, be cautious about believing that your loved one's troubles are your fault. Job's friends went to great lengths to pin fault on him, claiming that his loss was due to personal sin. God, however, declared more than once early in the book that Job was a righteous man. His friends were misguided.

Though our relationships are far from perfect, it is unlikely that your loved one's issues are your fault. Why not ask God to speak to you about this and set the record straight? That is his role, not ours.

Dear Father,
You are all-wise and your insight is perfect. I humble myself before you and pull back from opinions where I have gone too far. Help me rest in you. My insight is so limited, but I want to understand. Show me your purposes for what is transpiring in regard to my loved one. I trust you to do in my loved one what I cannot. Give me wisdom to do what I ought to do.
In Jesus's name, amen.

ENTERING INTO CHRIST'S COMPASSION
Day Three
Read John 6:1–14

Jesus then took the loaves, and when he had given thanks, he distributed them to those who were seated. So also the fish, as much as they wanted.

—John 6:11

It had been a long day already and thousands of people were hungry. Having compassion on them, Jesus inquired of the disciples where they could acquire food for this multitude. They were taken aback. It was an impossible task, yet Jesus meant it to be done, though not by normal means.

He still does that, even in regard to our loved ones. It is helpful to understand in such situations what is our role and what is his.

Our role is to offer him what we have. In this case, the disciples brought to Jesus a boy's lunch: five small loaves and two fish. Though it was such a small gift, in the hands of Jesus it fed the entire multitude with food left over.

Similarly, we should not underestimate the gift of our unconditional love to our loved ones. Furthermore, we shouldn't think small of our need for steadiness in the middle their volatility, or think poorly of our faithful prayers. Our surrender to God and listening ear, both to our loved one and more importantly to God, matter. It is unwise to disparage our refusal to give up hope for our loved ones. Neither should we think small of our willingness to apologize. Only we can offer these precious gifts to God.

It is God's role to bring the increase and perform the miracle we can hardly envision. Only God can do that. Only he can open their eyes to see a different path than the one they are walking and get out of the rut they're in. God alone gives them understanding of why they do what they do. Only he can set them free from crippling bondage. He alone liberates them from depression and hopelessness and gives them a new beginning.

Our hope and prayer are that he will graciously do this and much more. We don't have to figure everything out but simply yield to him what we have and are. He does the rest.

Dear Father,
You do far more than all that we ask or think. You do this by your power alone and always for your glory. I yield to you the gifts I can give, gifts of my time and love, my prayers and faithfulness. Have mercy on my loved one and save them, O Lord. You take the ordinary and make it extraordinary. May my loved one see the miraculous in their life. Be glorified.
In Jesus's name, amen.

OVERCOMING OBSTACLES
Day Four
Read Luke 8:40–56

While he was still speaking, someone from the ruler's house came and said, "Your daughter is dead; do not trouble the Teacher any more." But Jesus on hearing this answered him, "Do not fear; only believe, and she will be well."

—Luke 8:49–50

Jairus was an anxious father with a very sick daughter. Like him, there are several things we will find ourselves pushing through in order to keep step with Jesus.

The first is respectability. A man in his position in the temple would have been too proud to chase Jesus down. Jairus, though, was desperate. Desperation gets us past passivity or worrying about reputation.

Second, delays happen along the road. Though Jesus went immediately with Jairus, a considerable delay was caused by an obscure woman who received healing instantly from Jesus without even asking for it. The delay was frustrating, as was the fact that she was healed so quickly. We wonder why our loved ones are still mired in their struggles while another receives immediate healing. We must push through all such delays and continue to trust God.

Third, people will speak our worst fears to us. In their insensitivity, they articulate things we wouldn't say ourselves, putting us to tears. They don't speak for God; we must push through that.

Coming to Jairus, after the delay, it was announced that his daughter had died. Jesus immediately told Jairus not to give in to fear but to continue to believe him.

Fourth, we must push through certain limits that in our minds mark the point of no return. In Jairus's case, it was death itself. Jesus brought the girl back from death. You will want to quit at times because all seems so hopeless. Yet we must push through and trust God. Jairus pushed through and in the end experienced the rich compassion of Christ, who healed his daughter. He received what he came for.

Jesus is attentive to the prayers of desperate parents for their loved ones. Though it is not given to us to predict outcomes, we can be confident in the goodness of God. What an invitation we have to present our loved ones to God in the name of Jesus!

Dear Father,
You are full of compassion. Have mercy on my loved one and save them. Thank you for building tenacity in me and deepening my determination. I desire very much that you would deliver my loved one, yet I lose heart quickly. I fix my eyes on you, knowing that you are trustworthy and always do good. Heal this one who is so precious to me.
In Jesus's name, amen.

RECEIVING HELP FROM GOD
Day Five
Read Psalm 121

I lift my eyes to the hills. From where does my help come? My help comes from the Lord, who made heaven and earth.

—Psalm 121:1–2

To be human is to need help. From infancy, though, it seems that we learn to be independent and strong, reluctant to acknowledge that we need help. Walking with a loved one who is addicted, however, is a strong reminder of our dependence. We feel our lack at every turn with so many dangers and constant reminders of our powerlessness to change things. We need help, but from where will it come?

Our help comes from the Lord. We might look to the hills or to anything that seems unshakable to stop the trembling in our souls, but the truth is that our help comes from the Lord—from the one who made the hills. His help is first of all personal to us, so personal that we can say, "My help comes from the Lord."

Perhaps we feel that God worries about the big things, but we're on our own with these smaller matters. Not so! He watches over your coming and going, now and forevermore, to the smallest of details.

Second, he is ever-present, never dozing off. Though we drop off to sleep, he remains alert. This is a reminder that our work is only a subset of his, for while we sleep he continues to work. He watches over our loved ones even while we rest.

Lastly, he is well able to watch over all who trust in him. Though there are many things we don't understand on this unwanted journey, we know that he constantly wards off threats in the daily course of life and stands guard over our loved ones, as he does us.

All that is left is for us to trust him to be our help. We can trust him to help us in sorrow, loneliness, and every difficulty. The peace of God will guard our hearts and minds. Surely, he watches over us and guides us. Yes, he is with us. Be encouraged, for you are never alone.

Dear Father,
Thank you that I am never alone. Thank you for your constant presence with me. Thank you for walking with me every day and for your mercy, which is new every morning. Give me strength to keep going and never give up. You are my help and I call to you today, as I do every day. Come to my aid, Father! I need your touch in my life and the life of my loved one. Thank you.
In Jesus's name, amen.

ABOUT THE AUTHORS

Bill and Donna are parents of four adult children and grandparents to nine grandchildren. They have pastored at Toronto Alliance Church for twenty-nine years. They share a passion for the marginalized and have seen God do many wonderful things among them in the building of a church in the heart of the city.

Bill and Donna are both speakers at events and in churches. They speak passionately about prayer, the deeper life, and the poor.

Donna is the author of two other books, *Confessions of a Not so Average Girl* and *Confessions of an Unlikely Pastor's Wife*. Her website is donnaleadyck.com and her blog is called "Don't Forget Fridays" where weekly she reflects on important truths we need to remember.

ABOUT THE ARTIST

Bärbel Smith is a Canadian by heart and German by birth. Her fondest memories were growing up along the shores of Lake Huron and in the woods of Muskoka. Here she spent numerous hours with her sketchbook and paints, capturing the fascinating Canadian landscape. Later she lived in western Canada and received her training through self-study and attending the Alberta University of the Arts.

Since then, she has travelled from coast to coast capturing the colours, light, and joy in her depiction of the Canadian landscape, focusing on the emotive use of colour and line and erasing extraneous details and infusing her paintings with a God-inspired vision. Numerous layers of glazing give her paintings a glow, as if they were lit from within. She is a juried signature member of two national art organizations, is represented by several galleries, and currently resides in a country home surrounded by forest where she paints full-time.

Bärbel Smith SCA, OSA, AFCA
Contemporary Canadian Landscape Artist
289-251-2363
Website: www.barbelsmith.com
Email: barbelsmithartist@gmail.com
Instagram: www.instagram.com/barbelsmithart
Facebook: www.facebook.com/barbelsmithartist
Twitter: https://twitter.com/BarbelSmith